"In *Authentic,* Bill Barrett has written a gracious tribute to his father that also serves as a masterclass in how to live and work with integrity and purpose. It replaces the modern noise of productivity life-hacks with timeless values like showing up, staying curious, and always leaving others better off. Want to build a life that truly matters? Then this is a book to live by."

—Dan Sullivan, Cofounder of Strategic Coach

AUTHENTIC

An Old-School Approach to Building a Full Life, a Successful Business, and Real Relationships

WILLIAM S. BARRETT

*Story*BUILDERS PRESS

*To my father, Dave Barrett Jr., and my mother, Catherine
Barrett, whose stories grace the pages of this book and
whose legacies and fingerprints are all over the success I
have been blessed to enjoy in life and in business. They set
the foundation and set my compass on a certain course.*

*To my fiercely loyal wife, Jen, who every day
shows grace, courage, and strength beyond what
I am capable of, even on my best day.*

*And to my children, Julia and Billy, who provide me
with the greatest joys and moments of my life and have
always generously shared their time with me and allowed
me to be a hero to as many people as possible.*

CONTENTS

Introduction: Father to Son 1

Chapter 1 Outwork Everyone 19

Chapter 2 Overcome Setbacks 35

Chapter 3 Never Stop Learning 51

Chapter 4 Bet on Yourself 67

Chapter 5 Make Business Personal 81

Chapter 6 Develop an Abundance Mindset 97

Chapter 7 Share Your Time 111

Chapter 8 Be Present 125

Chapter 9 Play the Long Game 137

Chapter 10 Leave a Mark for Others 153

Note of Gratitude 171

About the Author 175

My First Holy Communion, looking up to my dad as I always did

FATHER TO SON

*Hard Work, Persistent Growth,
and a Commitment to Investing in Others*

I remember seeing my dad regularly pull all-nighters when I was a kid. It wasn't an occasional thing either. In fact, I'd wager that he rarely got more than four hours of sleep each night for much of his adult life. Whatever he needed to do for his family, his clients, and the people he cared about most—he always found a way to make it happen. He wasn't going to leave for the day until everything was done right. He'd come home exhausted, get a few hours of rest, and wake up to do it all again the next day.

As odd as that sounds, it never came as a surprise to me. That was just Dad—hard work, resilience, and a life marked by helping others. That's who he was.

But it wasn't until years later that I realized the level of impact my dad's commitment had on the people around him. At his funeral, a man I didn't recognize approached me with tears in his eyes. *Was this a childhood friend or an old Air Force buddy I had yet to meet?* The man made his way over to me and introduced himself.

"My name is Greg Peck. I'm so sorry for your loss."

As soon as he said his name, I instantly knew who it was—not the Hollywood actor Gregory Peck but the former general counsel of Corning Glass. I had never met him, but I remembered hearing his name as an old client of Dad's. Greg had long since retired, yet he had driven three and a half hours to make it to the funeral.

What would inspire somebody to do that for an old business contact?

Greg didn't drive more than three hours to come to the funeral just because my father did his job well. Dad's dedication went far beyond business. Greg told me that even after he retired, my dad would still drive to Corning and take him and his wife to dinner on Dad's own dime.

It made a lasting impression on Greg. After he retired, all the other professionals he had done business with throughout his career completely forgot about him. When he wasn't a big shot anymore and was no longer of use, they all disappeared—but not my father. He was the one guy who showed that he valued Greg as a person—not just as a means to an end.

That kind of consistent, intentional investment in people made my dad the man he was, and it made an impact on everyone he met. Paired with his incredible work ethic and unwavering resilience, he touched people's lives in a way I can only describe as transformational.

Talking to Greg Peck at the funeral crystallized something I had long thought to be true. I realized then that the character and philosophy my dad carried with him every day of his life weren't typical. They left an impact. In fact, they were what set him apart, made him successful both personally and professionally, and defined his legacy.

It's the reason his clients kept coming back to him time after time, even when larger and more prestigious companies threatened the viability of his business. Dad *worked harder* and *cared more* than anyone else. A lot of people can say they work hard, but he amplified that hard work with sincere *care.* He led with a giving hand. He made his clients his friends, and they fought for him in return. The principles he lived by defined his legacy and not coincidentally also made him successful.

And that brings me to you.

This book is about the intersection of my story and my dad's, but most importantly it's about a set of principles that have stood the test of time. In the chapters that follow, I'll share the philosophies that enabled my dad to push past the impossible and successfully reset his career even when all seemed lost. They're the same lessons that have also given me success. They're what helped me become the CEO of one of the top law firms in New Jersey and what shaped me into the kind of person my clients want to know, talk with, do business with, and be friends with.

Whether you're a business owner, a professional, or simply an individual who wants to build a successful life grounded in purpose, this book is for you. The person I am today, both personally and professionally, has been shaped by these principles. I can attest that they're the key to life success, enjoyment, fulfillment, and legacy—if you're willing to follow them.

It's a story I love to share, and it's a story I hope you'll love to read.

AN EARLY FOUNDATION

The lessons I learned from my dad were lessons he learned from honest experience. His family roots trace back to coal miners in Scotland, and the poor but hardy Scottish stereotypes couldn't be truer for our family tree. Dad often told stories about how he and his siblings cut up cardboard boxes and put them in the bottoms of their shoes with holes worn through them. The cardboard helped the shoes last just a little longer when they couldn't afford to buy new ones. The family didn't always have the money, but they were determined to find ways to get by.

Dad was one of four children, and one of them had Down syndrome. I can only imagine how hard it was for his parents to raise a child with special needs in that era while also trying to put food on the table.

He used to say, "We were poor, but we never went to bed hungry."

Then he'd pause and add, "Well, sometimes we went to bed hungry."

My grandparents immigrated to America from Scotland when they were teenagers, and Dad was born and raised in the Bronx in New York City. His father worked as an elevator operator and also as the superintendent of their apartment building. As you might expect, being an elevator operator didn't pay much, and being a building superintendent didn't pay anything. The only upside to the job was that they were provided a place to live in the building.

Still, the family had to constantly run on all cylinders just to make ends meet—and that included my father. Thankfully, he learned to be handy by watching his father manage their building. As a result, Dad could build or fix just about anything. According to him, he could never remember a time in his life when he didn't have a job. When he was about eight years old, he got a job delivering laundry for a Chinese laundromat while also running a shoeshine box. From that point on, he was always doing something to make money.

Those experiences shaped my dad as a person and in turn shaped me.

Hard work was the only thing Dad knew. There was no alternative. His life experiences taught him that if you want to succeed at anything, there's no other way to do it than by working hard. You roll up your sleeves and make it happen. He persisted despite obstacles, which paved the way for his success. And even when he didn't have much, he got joy out of giving what he did have to others.

He never sat me down and told me these values; he didn't have to. They were clear from the example he set and the way he lived his life—work hard, be persistent about your growth, and commit to investing in others, and the rest will follow.

HARD WORK

As kids, we tend to learn far more from what our parents do than from what they say. That was certainly true for me. My dad taught me the value of hard work by modeling it for me. He walked the walk just as much as he talked the talk.

I didn't know it until after I became an adult, but as a kid, my dad was apparently a real hothead. He got into a lot of fights and even got arrested on more than one occasion. As a teenager, he was brought before a judge and given two options: either go to jail or volunteer his services for the United States and serve his country in the Air Force. Dad hadn't yet finished high school, and getting a GED was part of the requirement to "choose" the Air Force opportunity. So he took the test, earned his GED, and then joined the Air Force during the Korean War. His childhood had already taught him to be industrious, but the Air Force taught him discipline and responsibility.

When Dad returned to the States, he went through a series of jobs, trying to get by. He tried his hand at being an actor, a photographer, and even a New York City cab driver, but nothing seemed to pan out. He'd often talk about how desperate he was just to have food to eat during those times. He didn't have pots or pans, but on one occasion he was so desperate to eat that he bought a can of Chef Boyardee, cut off the lid, and tried heating it right on the stove. He didn't realize the heat would make the food expand. Before he knew it, the pasta started spilling out over the top of the can and onto the stove. You can imagine my hungry father freaking out as he tried to salvage the pieces all over the stovetop. After all, it was all he had to eat.

Thankfully, Dad never gave up. He eventually got a job working as a janitor in a building in New York that housed a financial printing company. One day, while cleaning toilets, he heard some guys in the restroom talking about the fact that some union jobs were opening up to become pressmen. This was a chance for upward mobility in the business. So he asked the shop foreman, "Hey, who do you have to talk to for those jobs?"

The next thing Dad knew, he was meeting with the manager of the print shop and starting work as an apprentice. Keep in mind that operating hot lead printing presses wasn't an easy gig. The process involved casting melted lead into movable types—hot, heavy, and dangerous work. It required speed and accuracy, but he wasn't afraid of a little hard work. He didn't have any prior experience with printing, but he knew how to be handy since his father was a building superintendent. One thing led to another, and Dad soon earned his union card and became a pressman. He knew he wanted more for his life, and he wasn't afraid to put in the effort to get there.

That was just the beginning.

PERSISTENT GROWTH

A second core principle I learned from my dad is persistent growth, which to him meant being a lifelong learner, a risk-taker, and an overcomer. Dad was determined to always better himself, despite whatever obstacles came his way. He was committed to doing something with his life, and his growth didn't end there. Thankfully, my mom believed growth was possible too.

The night before my parents' wedding, my dad's own father warned my mom to call it off. "He's a bum," he told her. "He's never going to amount to anything." In his mind, my dad was a failure. He'd failed at high school (a GED wasn't a diploma, and the choice between the Air Force or jail wasn't something to brag about); he'd struggled to make ends meet with his low-paying jobs; and he couldn't figure out a path to a respectable life. My grandfather didn't have a great opinion of his son. But thankfully, my mother wasn't deterred from going through with the wedding. The outcome? She was rewarded with three kids and forty-six enjoyable years with my dad before he passed away.

Dad had worked hard to go from being a janitor to a pressman, but he still wanted more for his life. As he watched the men in suits going in and out of the print shop office, he thought to himself, *I have to get in there.*

But moving from being a pressman to a proofreader came with risks. To become a proofreader, Dad had to be willing to take a financial cut and give up his union card, which meant a loss of job security.

His union friends thought he was nuts. "Are you out of your mind? You're a poor kid from the Bronx. Why would you *ever* give up your union card? You've got job security and good benefits. Why risk it all?"

But my father wasn't the kind to settle. He wanted to become like one of the guys in the office—achieving that phase of his life's evolution. So if it meant assuming some risk and taking a calculated step backward to get a shot in the office, that's what he was going to do.

Of course, becoming a suit required first *owning* a suit, which my dad did not. So he went to the cheapest store he could find and bought two suits—a blue corduroy suit and a brown corduroy suit—and with those he managed to get a proofreading job.

But there was another obstacle in his way. Dad learned that to get where he wanted to go, he needed a college degree. But by that point, he was married with a couple of kids. He was now responsible for paying a mortgage and putting food on the table, which made going to school full-time out of the question.

So he studied part-time for eight years to get his degree, all the while commuting from New Jersey to New York City to work the third shift in the print shop. His daily routine for those eight years was attending William Paterson College in

New Jersey in the afternoons and then driving into the city and working at the print shop throughout the night. In the morning, he would leave the city and head back to New Jersey. But instead of going straight home, he would go to the bus depot and drive the morning bus for one of the local schools to make extra money. After all that, he would go home and fall asleep for however long he could. As my older siblings came home from their school each day, Dad would be heading out to *his* school to do it all over again.

By his sheer determination, Dad pulled it off. He got his degree and made his way up the ladder—from janitor to pressman, to proofreader, to customer service representative, to customer service manager, to nighttime manager, to daytime manager. Eventually, he went into sales, reasoning that salesmen had an unlimited ability to earn. And after thirty-five years, he was named senior vice president of the company. My father had worked his way to the top of the ladder.

During those thirty-five years, he was constantly improving himself at each step. For instance, one morning as I was getting ready for school, I heard a noise coming from the basement. "Read . . . Roger . . . rent . . ."

The first time I heard it, I thought, *What the heck is that?* I went down the stairs to take a look in the basement, and there was my dad. He had a book, and he was learning how to say his R's correctly. He'd grown up in the Bronx, so he had a strong New York accent. At some point along the way, he must have concluded that it made him sound unsophisticated and that people might assume he was unintelligent as a result.

But instead of complaining or feeling sorry for himself, he learned how to take ownership of his life and improve his situation. Over time, he totally eradicated his New York accent. In his mind, that was just one part of a journey of constant, never-ending improvement.

My dad was a man of many talents, and one of them happened to be spearfishing. Once I was driving with him on our way to a spearfishing tournament in Rhode Island when I looked over to see tears streaming down his face. He was a pretty tough guy—an Air Force veteran *and* a Scotsman—so this was definitely out of the norm.

I asked him, "What's the matter, Dad? Are you okay?"

He responded, "I'm okay, pal. You probably wouldn't understand it now, but someday you might." He kept his eyes on the road.

"What do you mean? What won't I understand?" I asked.

"Well," he said, "I just couldn't help but think that I just made more money this year than both of my parents earned combined in their entire lifetimes."

He paused and added, "And you know, it would have been nice for my dad to see it."

He wasn't making millions of dollars or anything like that, but he had worked his way to making a few hundred thousand dollars, which was more than his parents ever had. My grandfather had been incredibly hard on my dad, and he'd passed away while Dad was still struggling to get by. More than anything, Dad wished his father could have seen him reach this level of success.

Of anyone I know, my father certainly would have had the right to complain about his situation—*working two jobs, raising a family, and going to school at the same time.* It had to have felt like a herculean task. But he always approached his station in life from a position of gratitude and optimism—and in time, his persistence paid off.

A COMMITMENT TO INVESTING IN OTHERS

The third principle I picked up from Dad is the one that best defines his legacy: his commitment to investing in other people. Dad showed other people a level of care that's unmatched—in the ways he made business personal, in his generosity, in his ability to make people feel like they were the only person in the room, in his thoughtful questions, in his collaborative spirit, and even in his ability to disagree respectfully.

One of the places Dad did this most clearly was in the workplace. The print shop where he worked was in the business of financial printing. There's a good chance you don't even know what that is since everything has gone digital these days, but back in the day, banks and other financial institutions hired financial printers to produce millions of documents to maintain regulatory standards.

At that time, the law required publicly owned companies to provide their shareholders with all their written financial disclosures and annual reports—even for individuals who owned only one share of the company's stock. So for a large company with millions of shareholders, you can only imagine the level of stakes associated with winning their financial printing contract.

As you might expect, the competition to get another company's business for financial printing was extremely cutthroat—even within your own company. Everyone was vying for the commission and their piece of the pie. "Well, I know their lawyer." "Well, I know their investment banker." "Well, I know an executive at the company, and that's why we got their business." It was ruthless.

Meanwhile, my dad made it his mission to mentor younger salespeople who were trying to find their way. He'd spend time with them, teaching them how to do things the right way and how to service the clients, even though they were technically *his* competition. Instead of competing with the coworkers beside him who were trying to get the same account he was, Dad took the time to show them the ropes. It was unique then, and I'd argue that it's still unique today. But he enjoyed it. He felt that he got more out of life by being a hero to others than by focusing solely on his own needs.

"Where are you going?" my mom would ask him as he headed out the door on a Saturday morning.

"I'm going to help a friend renovate his bathroom" or "I'm going over to the neighbors' to help them build their deck," he would answer.

My mom was very aware of the dozens of projects that needed to be finished around the house, yet here was Dad being quick to say yes to others who needed help. Mom was peeved. She'd scowl and roll her eyes at him. But he would shrug it off, throw his tool belt over his shoulder, and head out the door.

Thankfully, Mom was cut from the same cloth, so ultimately she accepted that was just how things rolled with Dad. As I like to say, she was the person who took in all the stray cats—not in a literal sense, but she was the person others knew they could come to in their hour of need. Whether you were on the outs with your parents or literally running from the cops, if you knocked on the Barretts' door at 2:00 in the morning, she'd say, "Come in. There's a place to sleep in the basement. I never saw you here."

Needless to say, the environment I grew up in was marked by generosity, even though we didn't have much money to give.

Dad didn't reach any kind of real financial success until later in his life, but he was always generous with his time and the resources he did have. In my view, that's the real measure of a person. If you have a lot of money, are living in financial freedom, and don't have to worry about your next paycheck, writing some checks for charity is a nice thing to do. But it probably doesn't mean quite as much—mostly because it doesn't cost you quite as much. What speaks volumes is when you generously give a resource that you have in limited supply.

For most people—my dad included—time is the most valuable resource they have. Between working multiple jobs, studying for college, raising a family, and teaching himself daily, he was certainly short on time. There's no question it was the most limited and the most valuable thing he had to offer, yet he offered it freely. *Why is that?*

As I've gotten older, I've tried to reflect on why I do the things I do. Why do I get involved in some of the things I get involved in? Why do I take on some of the tasks I do? Over time, I've realized that a lot of it has to do with the joy I get from being a hero to others. My dad was a hero to so many people around him because of the way he consistently gave, and it paid off by giving him a life of meaning and a powerful legacy that will outlast him.

So whether it's a client, my spouse, my children, or my community, I want to be a hero to others in the same way my father was. It's why I served on my town council, coached sports, and mentored younger attorneys in my firm. I enjoy helping others succeed, and simply put, I get a thrill out of being a hero to other people.

Today, I get so much joy out of helping younger associates and partners grow and watching their careers elevate. I have seen them go from making a fair market base salary to achieving income levels far above what they ever imagined, and I can't help but think about how my dad must have felt when he saw my career soar. Achieving for yourself is one thing, but seeing those you've helped go on to achieve is another feeling altogether.

As I look back on my own life, it's easy to see the impact my father made on me. The way he lived left marks—fingerprints on success—all over the person I have become. Dad was a hero to so many people, and it gives me joy to be able to share him now with you.

FINGERPRINTS ON SUCCESS

I often find myself looking in the mirror, questioning how I got where I am. *What led me to the place I stand today? How did I end up becoming the CEO of one of the biggest law firms in the state? Am I still the kid from the working-class neighborhood I grew up in?*

I'm flooded with feelings of both disbelief and gratitude—and rightly so. I can't take all the credit. I owe almost everything that makes me who I am to my dad and my mom. I don't think they were setting out to raise a future CEO. They believed I could achieve whatever I set out to do, but they had no idea where my path would take me.

Yet it's been the principles my dad modeled that have become the manual for life that brought me here. The values I've picked up—hard work, persistent growth, and a commitment to investing in others—have paved the way for my success. By following the principles he lived by, I've traced his fingerprints on success.

I sometimes question whether I make a bigger deal out of these principles than they really are. But the more I look around, the more I see that they—and the Old-School Lessons for Life I've drawn from them—are universal truths that can serve everyone both personally and professionally.

As I reflect on the most successful business leaders and entrepreneurs I've worked with throughout my career, it's clear that these lessons are the common threads tying them all together. The lessons aren't complicated, and they're not flashy—but they are *powerful.* And in a world where so many people are hungry for direction in both their work and personal lives, a little bit of time-tested wisdom can go a long way.

If they can raise a kid like me from a working-class neighborhood to a leader in his profession, I can only imagine the kind of effect they can have on others who choose to pick them up and carry them with them through life.

In the pages ahead, I'll unpack ten Old-School Lessons for Life that have paved the way for my successes. In the process, you'll get a sense of my story and the person I've become by following these lessons. More than that, however, you'll learn how to create life success for yourself, discover what fulfills you, and build a legacy of impact—if you're willing to try them for yourself.

OLD-SCHOOL LESSONS FOR LIFE

Hard Work

1. Outwork Everyone
2. Overcome Setbacks

Persistent Growth

3. Never Stop Learning
4. Bet on Yourself

Investing in Others

5. Make Business Personal
6. Develop an Abundance Mindset
7. Share Your Time
8. Be Present
9. Play the Long Game
10. Build a Legacy for Others

With Dad in the Rotunda at University of Virginia

Chapter 1

OUTWORK EVERYONE

The Value of Hard Work

People who grew up in difficult environments often go in one of two directions. On the one hand, they might repeat the behaviors of their parents. Without even realizing it, they model what they grew up seeing. If their parents were hard and unemotional toward them, they may act similarly toward their children. On the other hand, people who had tough home lives may swing like a pendulum in the opposite direction of their parents. They realize they *don't* want the same kind of relationship with their children, so they decide to do something different. They break the cycle.

Thankfully, my dad chose option number two. My father didn't really share the specific details of how his own father spoke to him. But I know my grandfather was a hard man who was quick to point out Dad's shortcomings and not quick to offer encouragement or praise. As a result, my dad was left convinced that his father didn't think he'd ever amount to much in life.

Though my grandfather never got to see it, my dad proved him wrong. Dad worked his tail off, day in and day out. He put in years of tireless effort and built a life he was proud of. And he made sure to project a different sort of message to his kids. *You're capable of success. If you're willing to put in the work, you will amount to something great and accomplish anything you set your heart on.*

Conceive it, believe it, achieve it. It's not a message my dad even had to tell us outright. He showed us this was true by his attitude and the way he lived his life every day.

Dad didn't start out with a good deck of cards. In fact, it would have been incredibly easy for him to just complain and whine about his lot in life. Frankly, very few of his friends made it out of the neighborhood.

But my father didn't make excuses. He woke up every morning with the knowledge that he was born in the greatest country in the world—a place where you can get an education and do whatever you want to do. You don't get that opportunity everywhere. Simply being born an American puts you three steps ahead in the race of life. This knowledge made Dad grateful—grateful to have the opportunity to work hard, to get things, to have a job. It's why he loyally remained at the same printing company for more than thirty-five years.

Dad's posture of gratitude left no room for complaining about life being unfair. His philosophy was that he had been given the opportunity to do something with his life, and he wasn't going to waste it. When you are lucky enough to come from a place of privilege—which to him meant being born American—you have a responsibility to use it well, to make something of yourself, and to help other people in the process.

It's a lesson Dad taught me from a young age. Whenever I felt like I was being treated unfairly, he didn't try to swoop in and shelter me from it. Instead, he let those hard circumstances teach me how to deal with the real world.

Yeah, life's not fair. *It's hard.* But the only way to handle it is to *work hard* in spite of your perceived injustice. When you're facing adversity, you deal with it head on. When you have tough bosses, mentors, customers, or clients, you learn to cope with them, win them over, and recruit them as allies. That kind of coping is a learned skill, and it's developed through real-world practice.

If, for example, I felt like I wasn't getting enough playing time in a team sport, Dad didn't call the coach and complain. He didn't get me switched to another team. He knew that sticking it out would make me tougher if I could learn to hear the hard feedback, accept it constructively, and discover how I could become better as a result.

If I wasn't getting the playing time I wanted, that was on me. But it didn't have to be that way. The solution? *Outwork everyone. Make the case so compelling that the coach had no choice but to play me.*

Instead of complaining about not getting enough playing time, I worked my way to becoming a star player. In time, I reaped the rewards. When I committed to working harder than everyone else, the coach didn't have a choice but to see my value.

THE DANGER OF COMPLACENCY

Once you learn to outwork everyone, you're empowered to overcome whatever bad hand you've been dealt and whatever challenging obstacles come your way. But the inverse is also true. When you fail to see just how integral hard work is to your success, you become stuck in place.

People choose not to work hard for any number of reasons. Some struggle with a sense of direction, so they choose not to apply themselves in any direction at all. Others know intellectually that hard work is the key to success, but they're impatient. They work hard for a little while but give up when they don't see quick results. Some people choose not to outwork everyone because they are comfortable where they are. The cost-benefit analysis tips toward maintaining the *status quo*, and they decide to settle for "good enough."

What these people don't realize is that only putting in the minimum effort costs a lot more than they think. *Real success doesn't happen without hard work.*

When you don't work hard, you miss opportunities. You remain stagnant, watching as other people move right past you and achieve the things you want. Your skill development plateaus, and you become increasingly irrelevant in the ever-changing world around you.

Not only does this apathy hold you back professionally, but it affects how you think about yourself. Knowing you have a strong work ethic buoys your sense of self-worth and self-esteem. But without it, your confidence and feelings of adequacy can quickly erode. In time, you begin to lose respect for yourself as guilt and regret begin to take over your thoughts.

Take a moment to think about the people you admire and consider successful. They didn't get where they are by chance. If you look closely, running among these individuals is an invisible common thread: *They worked their tails off to get where they are.*

"Wait a minute," you might say. "What about the people who are just given everything on a silver platter or the people who stumble their way into success? What about the ones who inherit everything they have or who hit it big on the lottery? They never had to work hard, yet they seem to be sitting pretty."

I'm not trying to say that factors like privilege or luck don't play a part. It's a lot easier to become successful when you start with major advantages. But those factors only help you *get* to the top of the mountain. The hard part is *staying* there—and if you're not willing to put in the work, then privilege and luck alone won't keep you there. In that respect, hard work becomes the great equalizer.

More often than not, wealthy heirs and lottery winners waste what they have because they don't have the work ethic needed to maintain success. There's a reason why 70 percent of wealthy families lose their wealth by the second generation and 90 percent lose it by the third. It's the same reason nearly a third of lottery winners eventually declare bankruptcy. *Sustainable success only happens as the result of sustained hard work.*

STICKING TO THE GRIND

Outworking everyone is a slow grind. It requires patience. Success doesn't happen overnight; it's the outcome of consistent effort applied over time.

That's a pattern I've seen play out throughout my life. What most people don't know about me is that when I first applied to law schools, *I didn't get accepted anywhere.*

When people look at me, they see a bachelor's degree from Boston College, a law degree from a top-ten law school at the University of Virginia, work experience at a worldwide firm, and a managing partner title at one of the largest firms in New Jersey. What they don't see is all it took for me to get there.

After my low LSAT scores didn't get me into any law schools the first time around, I worked for a year and applied again. The second time, I only got into *one* accredited law school—and it was one on the lower end of the rankings.

What's more, they didn't even accept me outright. Instead, they put me into a trial admissions program where I had to go in the summer and take a handful of classes. If you got a B or better in every one of the classes, you qualified to enter the first-year class.

That was my only option, but it didn't matter. I had my foot in the door. I remember thinking, *Okay, I can work with this. I'm going to work really hard. I'm going to do well in the trial admissions program. And I'm going to get entered in the first-year class.*

And that I did. I had a chip on my shoulder the size of Texas, and I was ready to prove myself. I remembered Dad's example to outwork everybody, and I swore to myself that I was going to outwork every person in that school. It didn't matter how long I had to lock myself in the library. It didn't matter if I had to work myself like a dog. I was going to finish at the top of my class and transfer to one of the top ten law schools in the United States. *There's not a doubt in my mind,* I told myself. *I am 100 percent going to be attending a top-ten law school next year.*

I'm a reasonably smart guy, but I'm not the smartest guy in the world. I needed to work harder than everyone else if I wanted to set myself apart. So I made sure I was the last person to leave the library every day. I went to school, came home, exercised, ate something, took a shower, and went back to the library until it closed. I didn't go out. Come hell or high water, I was determined to get straight A's and finish at the top of my class. Nothing was going to stand in my way.

Another student named Pat who lived in my apartment complex was also an incredibly hard worker. To push myself harder, I made Pat my measuring stick. If I really wanted to outwork everyone, that meant I had to make sure I stayed at the library longer than Pat. Every day, Pat and I—along with my roommate Paul—were some of the last people to leave the library. And because we lived in the same apartment complex, I could tell whether Pat had already gotten home by looking at his window when I walked by.

Before long, it became a competition. When the weather was nice and he had his window open, I would yell, "Patty, you slacker! What time did you leave the library? Eight o'clock?"

In hindsight, it might sound a little crazy, but I knew one thing: I couldn't get where I wanted by waving a magic wand. The only way I was going to succeed was to outwork everyone. And in my case, a little healthy competition was just what I needed to make that happen.

In the end, I did it. In a class of well over two hundred, I finished at the very top. After my first year, I stuck to my word—I applied to most of the top ten law schools in the nation, and I started getting acceptance letters back in the mail one by one: Columbia, NYU, University of Virginia, and so on.

I decided I would go to the University of Virginia, and I didn't look back. When people at my first law school returned for year two, they asked Paul, "Where's Bill? I haven't seen him."

He responded, "Oh, you know, Bill finished at the top of our class. He got into a bunch of the top ten law schools, and he's at UVA now."

They looked at him incredulously. "No, seriously, come on. You're full of it. Where's Bill?"

Paul responded, "No, dude. He's at UVA right now." It wasn't until they didn't see me in class that they knew he was telling the truth.

I had made it to UVA, but my philosophy stayed the same. I kept working hard like my life depended on it, and it paid off. Before I graduated, I got an offer from one of the largest law firms in the world with offices in a dozen foreign countries. It was one of the hardest positions to get anywhere in the world, but since I had my sights set on it, I didn't let anything stop me from earning it.

Even when it came time to take the bar exam, I knew the only way to ensure success was to outwork everyone. I graduated from UVA on May 17. On May 18, I started my first bar review course, even though most of my friends told me they weren't going to start studying hard until after the Fourth of July.

Once again, I was married to the library. Over the next few months, I took two bar review courses and studied on my own every day. It was summertime, so the library closed earlier. But that didn't stop me. It just meant I had to find places in the school that were open just for students who were studying for the bar. I would find an open cubicle, hunker down there, and study until dinnertime. Then I would go home, have dinner, and get myself ready to do it all again. Every day, I repeated this routine. Nobody else was there because no one else was doing it.

But I said to myself, *I got this big job in New York where nobody fails the bar exam. I'm not going to be that guy, and I'll do whatever it takes to make sure of it.*

Once again, I did just that. I also took two state bar exams over the course of three days so I could practice in both New York and New Jersey. I passed them both and started my first job at one of the most prestigious firms in the world.

I went from being rejected everywhere to reaching the highest level of success possible for a first-year lawyer—all because I followed my dad's example and adopted the attitude he lived his life with:

I'm going to outwork you at everything.

You may outrank me.

You may outmuscle me.

You may outsmart me.

But you'll never outwork me.

THE UNSEEN THREAD

Now that I've reached some level of success in my life and career, I've caught myself being increasingly reflective about the things that have brought me to where I am. As I look at my own life and those of other successful people around me, I begin to notice one common, unseen thread that is present in every success story: *sustained hard work.*

Again, it's not complicated, and it's not flashy. But from my experience, I've come to see that it is vital.

Very few of the entrepreneurs who are wildly successful in this country are silver spooners. People don't just accidentally fall into success. They don't just figure out some idea that earns them a billion dollars without having laid substantial groundwork to get there. Sure, exceptions exist, just like there are people who've been struck by lightning. But it's just that—being struck by lightning.

Having represented more than a thousand successful people over the decades, providing legal counsel to business leaders and entrepreneurs, I've noticed that the most common trait of those at the top of their game is that they outwork their competition.

Those people work harder than everyone else in every respect. They are not lazy. They're passionate about their work, and they're determined to see it through. They commit to the long, sustained grind. And the groundwork isn't laid over one or two years either—it's ten or twenty years. The thread is everywhere, and there's no substitute for it.

In my own experience, I've found that hard work and a little elbow grease can make up for a lot of brain cells. In fact, I would wager that if you were to run IQ tests on the most successful people, a majority of them would turn out to be of relatively average intelligence. But because of their work ethic, they are able to make up for it.

Take, for example, my good friend Bernie. He's a really smart guy, but I think he'd be the first to tell you that he's no Albert Einstein. However, he does have great emotional intelligence and an unbelievable work ethic that he's sustained over time.

Today, Bernie is the CEO and chairman of one of the largest—if not *the* largest—executive coaching and practice management companies for doctors in the country. He has a house in Pebble Beach, California, drives a beautiful Ferrari, and by all accounts appears to be cruising through life.

But what people don't see is that for over thirty years, Bernie was the guy sleeping on planes and in hotels more than 200 nights a year. He sustained an exhausting pace for decades to get where he is today, demonstrating tremendous perseverance and an unmatched dedication to his business. What you see today didn't happen by accident. It's the intentional product of three decades of unbelievable grind, hard work, and gradual evolution.

This common thread is why my dad's example is universal. Whether you're an athlete, an entrepreneur, a job applicant, or anyone trying to work their way up the ladder, the solution is the same: *Make the case so compelling that they have no choice but to choose you.*

HARD WORK OVERCOMES

Your unwavering and sustained work ethic will make it so obvious that you're set apart from others that there's no ignoring you. The question isn't "What does the coach need to figure out so you can play, even though you haven't gotten better?" It's "What do I need to do to get better—to be a better player, worker, owner, or professional? How do I up my game to make the case clear and convincing?"

There are no shortcuts or casting blame. Whether or not you achieve success depends entirely on if you're willing to put in the work. The responsibility is squarely on your shoulders.

In the era of participation trophies, it's far too common to jump to the conclusion that the coaches, teachers, and bosses are wrong—rather than that you have room to improve. It's easier to blame everyone else for your shortcomings when you begin with the assumption that you have a right to it. The reality is that *you don't*.

In my view, this belief has made people lose their ability to cope with difficulties. In the real world, complaining about life being unfair doesn't get you anywhere. Jobs can be difficult. Clients can be difficult. School can be difficult. But a necessary life skill is learning how to navigate the difficult. Anybody can navigate the easy. But if you're only used to paddling downstream, you'll never develop the strength needed to fight the current.

There are stories upon stories of people who have fought the current and overcome bad hands because they learned to embrace the difficult and go the extra mile. Think of the athletes who stay on the field until the last hints of daylight are gone, trying to get just a little more practice in even after everyone else has left.

It's because hard work is the great equalizer that the most talented athletes aren't always the ones who get the most playing time. When individuals work harder than everyone else to make up for their inadequacies, they are capable of taking themselves to a higher level.

Hard work always wins.

HOW FAR YOU'VE COME

A word of warning: When you make it your goal to outwork everyone, it can be easy to focus entirely on how far you have to go and forget to appreciate how far you've come.

As I began making steps in my legal career, I often got discouraged when I looked at where I was versus where I wanted to be. But instead of obsessing over what I hadn't yet achieved, Dad always encouraged me to focus my attention on the places I had succeeded and the progress I had made. He'd tell me, "Bill, look at everything you accomplished this year. You should feel like a million bucks. Forget about what you didn't accomplish. Look at what you did accomplish, and keep building on your success."

I had to ask myself, *Why am I walking around disappointed right now?* It didn't make sense. By every metric, I was succeeding at a greater pace than others at my experience level. I was out-earning my peers, building relationships, and doing what I loved every day—helping people grow their businesses, overcome challenges, and achieve their goals. I was making increasingly more each year, gaining financial freedom, and enjoying a comfortable lifestyle. I had a great marriage and great kids. What was there not to be happy about?

I can't tell you how much my father's encouragement helped ground me in the early parts of my career. For most people, it's all too easy to focus on the gaps in their lives—the unmet goals and self-imposed expectations. But when you're only focused on the gaps, you forget to enjoy all the things you've worked so hard to achieve. Conversely, when you appreciate the payoff of your hard work, it gives you a positive motivation that pushes you and fuels you for more.

So as I kept working hard, I also focused on the things I had accomplished more than the things I hadn't. In time, that focus led to a snowball effect with real-world payoffs as each year's successes built upon the previous years' accomplishments.

I remember the first year my income surpassed a million dollars. I was sitting on the couch in my living room in front of the fireplace, alone on Christmas Eve, reflecting on all the things the year had brought me. As I sat there on that couch, tears collected in my eyes.

They were complicated tears. Part of it was being proud of what I had accomplished. I had invested so much and made so many sacrifices getting to that point in my career, and it was rewarding to see it all come to fruition.

At the same time, I was also thinking about my dad. I remembered the time I saw him cry in the car as he reflected on how much further he had made it than his parents. More than anything, he wished his father could have seen it because he knew his father never believed he could get there.

That night, I wished Dad had gotten to see how far I had come—but for a very different reason. I wished he had gotten to see me make it that far, precisely because he *always* knew I would get there. More than anybody, he'd have been the least surprised and the most proud. He did his job raising me. He taught me to work hard and outwork everyone—and he believed I was capable of doing it.

The same is true for you.

You're capable of achieving whatever goal you set out to accomplish. If you're willing to put in the work, you can realize your vision of success.

Dad and me, Chas. P. Young Appreciation
Fishing Trip in the early 1980s

Chapter 2

OVERCOME SETBACKS

Grit and Resilience

Hard work always pays off, but the journey to success isn't without its setbacks. Bumps in the road are a reality of life. There's no escaping them. In an imperfect world, things aren't always going to go according to plan. I'd go so far as to say that if there's one thing in this world you can count on, it's that you will inevitably face setbacks along the way.

That's a reality my dad learned the hard way.

As Dad made his way up the corporate ladder at his financial printing company—the Charles P. Young Company—it began after many years to feel like his star was finally rising. Every major competitor came knocking on his door saying, "Come on, have dinner with us. Let's talk. We want you to be the head of our sales department. We'll put you on the executive leadership team. We'll pay you this amount of money. We'll give you guarantees."

Regardless of the offers those companies put on the table, he stayed loyal to the Chas P. Young Company and to the people who gave him that initial opportunity twenty years earlier when he was still cleaning toilets. He would simply say, "Thank you, but I'm not interested."

But as fate would have it, a major setback was right around the corner. The year was 1990, and I was just about to start as an undergraduate at Boston College. My father had been making good money at his printing company and had gotten into investing. After decades of scraping by, he was beginning to finally feel some security and stability in his work. In fact, he had even made plans to pay for my college out of his income and savings. What he didn't know was that a Wall Street corporate raider was about to entirely pull the rug out from under his feet.

A Gordon Gekko–type raider had looked at the Chas. P. Young Company's balance sheet and realized that it had extremely valuable assets. The one-hundred-year-old printing company owned a large building in New York City on Varick Street, as well as corporate headquarters in cities such as Houston, Los Angeles, San Francisco, and Chicago. The company had no debts, and it owned significant real estate in all those major locations. It was more valuable on paper than it was in operation. Even though the company was making money, the divided assets were worth far more than the operating business.

So this raider did what Wall Street raiders do best. He bought the Chas. P. Young Company and liquidated it for its assets.

The next day, everybody showed up for work, only to find the proverbial lock on the door. *Dad's security?* Erased. *His pension fund?* Evaporated. *A stable income?* Gone. That was it. Thirty-five years down the drain.

At this point, my dad was in his mid-fifties. He had already put in his time outworking everyone to build a successful career. He had gone through the long progression from cleaning toilets to going to college at night, to becoming a top executive—only to then hit rock bottom unexpectedly. *How was he supposed to start from scratch at that age?*

Then again . . . *what other choice did he have?*

Following the liquidation, everybody from the company went scurrying to every other financial printing company in sight. But the companies that previously wanted to hire my dad weren't offering the same deals anymore. With the closing of the Chas. P. Young Company, there was a sudden surplus of talent. The competitors knew *they* had the leverage now.

Instead of getting discouraged and jumping on the first offer to come his way, my dad decided to pause and look at the bigger picture. He realized that there was a short lifespan left in the world of financial printing and that this setback might even be an opportunity for a positive change in direction.

Part of the job of financial printers was to produce annual reports for public companies that were legally required to provide these reports to every stockholder in the company. However, over time, these annual reports started to become more like company marketing pieces, including colorful covers, brochures, and promotional materials in addition to the financial data. All the companies that had been wanting to hire Dad were strictly financial printing companies, but Dad intuited that commercial printers who recognized this shift and diversified their offerings were the way of the future.

So he decided to go to a much smaller company that recognized this shift. However, they guaranteed him nothing but a $50,000 base salary. Above that, it was going to be all commission-based. But if he could pick up all his old customers, that should be no problem, *right?* Everything would be just as before—with the added benefit of now being able to do financial *and* commercial printing.

Unfortunately, it wasn't that easy. In the time it took my dad to find a job, the clients he was previously working with had gone elsewhere. They had started taking their business to the other big financial printing competitors, and Dad wasn't able to get all their business back.

On top of that, the economy took a turn for the worse, and he was making little more than his base salary. He had already overextended his finances when operating under his previous income, and now he was struggling not to go bankrupt. Meanwhile, Mom got a job as a clerk at Macy's to help make ends meet. When things got really thin, my parents even refinanced the house to help put me through college.

But my father was determined to claw his way back. He had climbed his way out of the hole before, and he knew he could do it again. For the next ten years, he put in the grind. Whatever it took, he was resolved to build himself back.

Once again, that meant making sacrifices. I remember before the Chas. P. Young Company closed, he would drive into New York City every day. But during the years after the shutdown, he stopped taking his car and started taking the bus into the city to save money. On days when it wasn't raining, Dad would sometimes even walk his thirty-minute commute from Port Authority to Midtown and forgo the subway to save that $1.50. If he knew customers were coming in and catering food, he would count on that for his lunch. Otherwise, he'd often wait to eat until he got home.

What amazed me most about my dad during this time was his positive outlook despite the circumstances. He was hopeful. Every time someone talked to him, he talked about opportunity. Even when things were slow, the first words out of his mouth were always about the business he was getting, the opportunities he was pursuing, and the people he was talking to.

It was never doom and gloom with Dad. He was always looking for the silver lining—and I think that's what got him through. At that age, most people would have said they'd never get back to where they were. But little by little, he built himself back.

When all seemed lost, the people he was loyal to showed loyalty in return. Three or four of Dad's close clients remembered how dedicated he was to them, and they convinced their companies to take up business with him once again. Friends like Greg Peck at Corning Glass found ways to give him some of their smaller jobs, which eventually led to opportunities for him to bid on bigger and bigger printing jobs.

In the end, Dad was closing multimillion-dollar deals and earning six-figure commissions. He was back. It took ten years—a decade—for him to regain his clientele and make it back to where he was. By that time, he was sixty-five years old. The journey to get there was a slow, painful, and difficult one, but Dad didn't see it that way. He made it back to the top because he looked at his setback and instead saw it as an opportunity.

The lesson? *The difference between a stumbling block and a steppingstone all depends on how you look at it.*

CHOOSING DEFEAT

Clawing his way back to the top may have been the greatest challenge of my dad's business life. But through it all, he always tried to stay positive and upbeat. In fact, I can only recall a single instance when the cracks truly started to show.

Dad was over at the little delicatessen down the street from our house that everyone called "The Lake Store." It was the place where all the locals hung out, got coffee or a bagel, and picked up their pack of cigarettes or the newspaper. While Dad was getting his coffee, he ran into a neighbor named Bob Connelly, a local union electrician. Since it was a small town where everyone knew everyone, Dad knew Bob pretty well.

Bob waved and asked him, "Hey, how are you doing?"

For whatever reason, my dad was feeling especially overwhelmed with the upheaval in his life that day, and he decided to let it all out on Bob.

"I'm doing okay," Dad started, "but the company I'd been with for thirty-five years went out of business. They raided the pension fund, and everybody lost their pension money. So now I don't have a pension anymore. On top of that, I had to figure out where I would work next. I started at a smaller company that I thought would be a good move, but a lot of the clients are preferring to use the bigger companies that I used to compete against, and . . ."

"Woah, buddy," Bob interrupted, "We've all got problems. I was just trying to make small talk and say hello."

As Dad would recount the story, that moment was his wake-up call. *What are you doing?* he asked himself. *This is so contrary to who you are.* As he walked away, he realized that he owed Bob a debt of gratitude for calling him out and making him realize what he was doing.

That day, Dad swore to himself that he'd never let himself get that way again. No matter what was going on, he wasn't going to let himself become a dark cloud, bringing everyone else down and sucking the life out of a room. Why? Because he realized the negative consequences that come when you respond to setbacks with whining and complaining rather than with grit and resilience.

Responding with negativity makes *you* feel lousy, and it brings down everybody around you—which can come with all kinds of consequences. When you respond with a defeatist attitude rather than with grit and resilience, you don't have the driving motivation to continue working your way back up the ladder. If your focus is on the losses behind you, you won't be able to see the opportunities ahead of you.

On top of that, when your negative attitude is bringing down everyone else, nobody wants to be around you. Whether you realize it or not, that negativity flows off of you. It doesn't matter who you are; you can't hide the toxic energy that you give off when you respond to challenges with negativity.

The consequences? You're the first person to be fired, demoted, or left off that big project you want to be put on. When the owner of your company is getting on a plane to go to an important conference, there's no way you're getting invited. You're no fun to be around.

As a customer or client, what kind of person would you rather do business with and spend time with? Would you prefer a person who has a contagious excitement for life or a person whose negative energy only drags you down?

THE DETERMINING FACTOR

Dad's example showed me that at the end of the day, you have the final say on how you experience whatever's coming at you. Of course, setbacks like the failure of a business venture or the loss of a job are major contributing factors to your life, but they don't have to be the determining factors. When my father's world was rocked by the biggest financial setback of his life, he didn't languish in his defeat or obsess over the downsides. He recognized that his response—his decision to be positive or negative—was *a choice*. And that choice made all the difference.

We're all human, so obviously there will be times when we feel disappointed. But that doesn't mean you have to wallow in your disappointment. Over the course of my life, I've tried to condition myself to acknowledge whenever I'm feeling disappointed without letting it keep me down for long. There's no point in living in defeat.

No matter what I do, I'll have to exert some energy in responding to the setback, so why not respond in a way that doesn't make me and the people around me feel terrible? If given the choice, why would I choose the option that does nothing but bring everyone down?

Setbacks are inevitable. It's a lesson I learned early on in my career—both from my dad and from my mentors in the legal profession. No matter what you do, you're going to lose clients, and you will lose them for many different reasons. Clients will retire, sell their businesses, or pass away. They will develop relationships with other people or give a friend a chance to handle their work. There's no avoiding it.

I remember one of my first major clients was a very well-known and successful oral surgeon named Dr. Zachary.

Although he was an oral surgeon professionally, he was involved in a number of different businesses and investments. I began representing Dr. Zachary with some small things here and there, but it wasn't long before he had me doing everything from corporate law to employment law to real estate law to estate planning. The work I was doing for the doctor included every imaginable thing a lawyer could do for a client, and I gave it everything I had to make it a transformational, long-term relationship. At a time when my book of business was under a million dollars, my work for Dr. Zachary made up about 20 percent of what I earned. I certainly wasn't going to let him down.

Then there came a time when Dr. Zachary decided to bring on a business partner, and he had me help structure the deal. I zealously advocated for Dr. Zachary and helped him produce an ideal agreement. I made sure the agreement was fair and balanced but also gave Dr. Zachary the best result from a business and tax perspective. Just a few months later, I received a phone call totally out of the blue. Dr. Zachary told me he really appreciated the work I had done for them in the past, but his partner felt they needed to jointly select someone new, and they no longer required my services. *I had been let go.*

It was a punch to the gut. My biggest client was gone *just like that.* I was devastated. How do you replace a client who constituted 20 percent of your revenue? None of my other clients even came close.

I had been knocked down—but definitely not knocked out. After the reality of the situation set in, I picked myself up and reminded myself what my mentors had told me: "Clients will come and go for all kinds of reasons, many of them will not be your fault. Your job is to keep restocking the shelves with new clients."

I had to brush it off and keep moving forward—no time for feeling badly. In my mind, the next great opportunity was just around the corner.

Around that time, I got involved in a young professional marketing group to make connections and learn how to grow my circle of influence. At the time, I didn't feel the immediate benefits of networking with other people who weren't necessarily at a mature stage in their career, but I was preparing myself for the better opportunities to come—learning how to sell myself, give an elevator pitch, and expand my center of influence. After all, you never know where your next invaluable connection is going to come from.

In time, that skill development paid off. I found new clients, restocked my shelf, and now have a book of business seven or eight times the size of what I had when I lost Dr. Zachary.

WHAT'S JUST AROUND THE CORNER

No matter what you've lost, the path to overcoming obstacles with grit and resilience is found by looking for the opportunities ahead of you instead of hanging your head in defeat. Whenever you face a setback, the question you ought to be asking yourself is this: "How can this be used to set me up rather than knock me down?" It's only when you start asking that question that you truly prepare yourself to take hold of what's next.

Later on in my legal career, my firm brought on an attorney who quickly became an incredible asset to our team. This attorney had previously worked as a practitioner in a small firm with only one partner. However, he had a broad base of knowledge and a real knack for intellectual property law.

Once he was with us, I connected him with one of my best clients, a privately held business that developed software. The client gave me the opportunity to pitch what other services the firm could do for him, and I brought our new attorney along with me. As luck would have it, the client's biggest need was for a good patent lawyer. This attorney was able to articulate all the problems and weaknesses in our client's current patent portfolio and show what a clear benefit he would be to their business. It was a match made in heaven, and over time, the client came to love working with this attorney. As a result, the relationship between the client and our firm grew. Eventually, we were averaging a million dollars a year in legal fees from this one client alone—more than five times the work we had done for my old client Dr. Zachary.

By that point, the now-not-so-new attorney was making upwards of half a million dollars a year in income, and his skills and numbers were only climbing. As a young guy having been lifted up from a relatively modest situation, he was grateful for the opportunity to be part of our firm. At the same time, he was becoming close friends with the owner of the tech company who kept dropping hints that he would love for our attorney to come work for him as their in-house general counsel. My colleague always replied that he appreciated the offer but was happy where he was at our firm.

One day, though, he made his way into my office and slumped down into a chair. He gave me a nervous look and said, "Our friend made me an offer again today."

"Oh?" I asked. "What was it this time?"

"Well, it's about a million dollars a year plus 2 percent vested equity in the company, which is currently valued at nearly three hundred million."

Woah! I took a long, deep breath. Was I losing a highly talented attorney, who at that point had also become a personal friend, *and* a multimillion-dollar client at the same time? How could I let them both go? But then again, what could I do about it? As a business, there was no way our firm was positioned to compete with that kind of offer. No matter what, we'd be taking a huge hit, but we'd recover. And honestly, it was the best thing for my friend.

"I'm going to take off my managing partner hat, put on my big brother hat, and be candid with you," I said. "You have to say yes. I don't want you to go, but I'd be lying if I told you not to take this deal. Even with as hard as you're working, I can't pay you that kind of money."

He told me he appreciated my honesty and that he was going to take the job. As he left my office, I reminded myself that I couldn't let this setback keep me down. *This just means it's time to restock the shelf,* I reminded myself.

I was prepared to take his leaving as a total loss, but I also knew the kind of guy he was. He was so grateful for our firm that he went out of his way to secure work for us while in his new position, suggesting to his new employer that our firm was still the best option for legal assistance and that our familiarity with the business and our ability to work closely with our former partner would be an advantage for the company. On more than one occasion, he put his own neck on the line to help us out. As a result, we didn't lose that work for many years, and I had time to continue to build up my client base so we never suffered a setback. Through it all, I kept my focus on the future and the continued growth of our organization—firm in my belief that our best days were yet ahead of us.

YOUR TIME WILL COME

The only way to persevere with grit and resilience is to have optimism or hope about the future. You have to believe that your time will come and that opportunity still lies ahead. Otherwise, you'll struggle to find the motivation to carry on.

This is a lesson I learned from watching my dad. It's a lesson I've lived out in my own life and one I've seen my son work through when he moved from middle school to high school.

As a middle school student, my son had an Individual Education Plan (IEP), which is essentially an individualized learning plan to help him navigate certain subjects. It was just what he needed at the time, but when students with IEPs move up in school, administrators often want to put them in easier classes so they don't fall behind or fail. The problem, though, is that the students don't get the chance to push their limits and prove themselves. In high school, they are less likely to have the opportunity to take advanced placement (AP) classes, which have become a prerequisite for the more elite academic universities.

My son was and still is an ambitious student and person. Even at that age, he already had dreams to go to an excellent college, and he knew that if he was put in the easiest classes, those schools would not likely consider him for admission. So he advocated for himself. He asked his counselor if he could take a higher math class.

"I know I can do it," I remember him saying.

But the school wouldn't do it. So he tried again.

This time, they agreed that if he went to summer school and passed the math class they wanted him to take freshman year with a B average or better, they would allow him into the harder course for the fall semester. And that's exactly what he did.

Summer school started a few days after classes let out and went five days a week, six hours a day, all the way to the end of July. Every day he took notes and studied, all so he could take a harder class. He learned an entire school year's worth of math in a matter of seven or so weeks. It was inspiring to see him sacrifice most of his summer and put in the hours of work it took to achieve his goal. At the end of the class, he sat for the exam and easily surpassed the requirement.

As of this writing, he's in his senior year of high school, has been a solid student, voluntarily gave up his IEP, and is committed to attend Boston College. Had he listened to the popular wisdom four years ago, his future might look very different. But he didn't. He battled for what he thought was right and what he knew he was capable of. He believed in himself that if he worked hard enough, he could make it happen.

The rest is history. He's graduating. He's going to Boston College.

Setbacks are inevitable, but you don't have to let contributing factors become your determining factor. Don't forget that your response is a choice. Choose to focus on the opportunities present in your challenges, and you'll be better prepared to respond with grit and resilience. Don't relent, and keep your head up. Your time will come—and when it does, be ready.

Family Weekend at Boston College, freshman
year, 1990, with Mom and Dad

Chapter 3

NEVER STOP LEARNING

Education Beyond the Classroom

My dad valued education like no one else, and he always pushed me to appreciate its value too. "Billy," he said, "one thing nobody can take away from you is your education. Nobody can take what's in your mind. Once you have it, it's yours."

Having come from a poor family, Dad had good reason to value his education. His scholastic opportunities weren't just given to him; they were hard-earned and came at a real cost. It wasn't easy going to school while also working two jobs and raising a family. But Dad saw firsthand the life-changing impact that an education could have on his life success. He saw in the business world that a lack of a degree barred him from accessing the higher-level positions he really wanted. Finally getting his degree not only gave him self-respect but also allowed him to kick down doors and elevate within his company. He was able to move up from positions that had ceilings in terms of opportunities, making his way to the highest ranks of the business. With that perspective, it's no wonder he always hammered home the value of learning.

But as much as my father valued his formal education, the importance he placed on learning didn't stop at the classroom. He was *intellectually curious*, wanted to know how to do everything, and read just about anything. Transcending school, he made being a lifelong learner part of a process of constant, never-ending improvement.

Even before self-improvement came into vogue with popular speakers and influencers such as Tony Robbins, Dad was already an avid fan. In our household, Zig Ziglar was *the guy*. Dad had dozens of Zig Ziglar cassette tapes and played them in the car to and from work every day. With personal development and growth as his goal, he made it his mission to learn how to think the right way with the right attitude and the right mindset.

Dad's mission of constant, never-ending improvement was practical too. Having been raised as the son of a building superintendent, he knew how to do a lot, but that didn't keep him from always wanting to learn how to do more. In fact, he had a whole series of books about every type of home improvement project imaginable. He wanted to be able to do everything himself, and he committed to learning how to make that happen.

As a result, when Dad wanted to put an addition on the house, he took out the permits, did the masonry work for the foundation, framed it, wired it, plumbed it, roofed it, sided it, and finished it all on his own.

On the weekends, Dad was always looking to make extra money, and he put his constant learning to good use. Whether it was putting in sheetrock, fixing a roof, or repairing HVAC units, he learned how to do just about everything.

His skillset didn't end with house repairs either. To make extra money, Dad took it upon himself to also learn how to work on cars. When he was driving a school bus in the morning and going to college at night, he would also wake up early on Sunday mornings to go to the Texaco station in the center of town and do brake and clutch jobs for the owner of the gas station.

I don't know how to describe it other than that my dad was obsessed with learning how to do everything. I don't think "resourceful" even comes close to covering it. To this day, I've never met another human who shared his inherent need to know how to do everything or his incredible ability to figure it out.

With time, I realized for myself just how valuable this hunger for learning is. It was the dead of winter, and I was living in my first house when my furnace decided to blow out. Right away, I instinctively called the HVAC company, which was prepared to charge me an arm and a leg to get it fixed in the emergency weather conditions. At the time, I was barely able to afford the place, but I didn't see any other option. "Eight hundred dollars? Fine. Just get me on the list."

I later called my dad to let him know about the furnace situation. "What?" he responded. "That's crazy! I can tell you right now that the problem is one of three things. It's either the thermostat, the motor, or the fan, and you can find them all at Home Depot for under a hundred dollars total. Cancel that appointment."

Classic Dad.

So I canceled my appointment, and he took a trip over to Home Depot. He brought the parts to my house and installed them on my furnace. He hit the switch, and the furnace started running again. "You owe me eighty dollars," he said with a laugh.

That kind of thing happened all the time. I once mentioned to my dad that I needed to get a new grill. Early the following Saturday morning, I was still lying in bed when I heard a noise out on my back deck. I looked outside the window and saw him lying on the deck, taking the grill apart.

"You know," he said in his typical fashion, "When a grill's not working, the problem is almost always the regulator."

This time, I couldn't help but laugh. In just a few minutes, he had it turning on again.

Even as Dad got older, he never lost track of his constant mission of lifelong learning and personal growth. "You might lose your ability to walk. You might lose your ability to hear.

You might lose your ability to see," he'd say, "but as long as your brain is still working, your education is one thing nobody can ever take away from you."

STAGNANT AND OBSOLETE

From the time I was young, Dad modeled for me how to appreciate the value of lifelong learning, but I'd argue that he's likely the exception to the rule. Especially as people get older, our unfortunate tendency is to become stuck in our ways and resistant to change. In short, we adopt a *fixed mindset* and say:

"It is what it is."

"You can't teach an old dog new tricks."

"I've never been good at that kind of thing."

"If you've got it, you've got it. If you don't, you don't."

Some people have struggled with new things in the past and don't want to experience failure again. They don't want to make mistakes, so they resolve to stay in their lane. Others don't want to learn simply because they're stuck in their ways and don't want to bother adjusting to change. They don't see the consequences of stagnation and conclude that things are good enough the way they are.

But the truth is, in a world that's constantly moving forward, stagnation means you get left behind. You become obsolete. Instead of keeping up with the current, you're dead in the water. I've seen this happen everywhere—even in my own profession and with lawyers I know personally.

For example, I've seen lawyers who started practicing in an era when professionals created documents and correspondence using dictation machines and had their secretaries type their messages for them. Although these are very smart and talented people, not all of them have been willing to grow and change. For years, some continued using dictaphones for all their correspondence, even past the point where they could get replacement parts or tapes for their machines.

Our IT guys tried to help accommodate them—setting them up with the modern-day equivalent of dictaphones so their messages could be digitally transcribed. But these lawyers' unwillingness to adapt and learn made them inefficient. They couldn't handle client matters with the same efficiency that others could. They were slow, expensive, and becoming increasingly obsolete.

As I like to say, "When you stop growing, you start dying."

That's a lesson my mentor, Mr. Mandelbaum, has discussed many times. He has often described his annual spring trip to Florida to visit old friends. Most of them are retirees who stopped working and stopped involving themselves in anything new. It might seem like the high life at first, but how many rounds of golf can you play before even that starts to get old? Then the next thing you know, you're one of those people who always hits up the early bird special and has nothing to talk about but your latest doctor's visit.

Mr. Mandelbaum is well into his eighties, but as a person committed to lifelong learning, he refuses to allow himself to become stagnant or obsolete. Whenever he makes a trip to Florida, after a few days he always seems to be itching to get back home.

"Bill," he says, "it's been a nice trip, but I am ready to get back home. Everyone here just keeps repeating the same old stories. They talk about their doctors' appointments, their golf games, and stories I have heard a hundred times by now. There's nothing *new* happening in their lives."

"Why would I ever stop working?" he asks. "I like what I do. I enjoy my clients and my partners. So long as I continue to be blessed with good health, I'm going to keep working—if only to be a mentor to other people and help them realize their goals and dreams."

The sad reality is that many people give up on learning new things far before they reach that age. They become stagnant and obsolete, and their stagnation only accelerates their decay. There's no escaping it: *When you stop growing, you start dying.*

GETTING OUT OF YOUR LANE

This past December, Mr. Mandelbaum turned eighty-nine. Every day he comes into work with a vibrancy and excitement for what lies ahead. He's always growing and learning, which fuels him with an incredible, life-giving energy. It's remarkable. We speak in person or on the phone nearly every day, and it is a time I look forward to and cherish. I just hope that when I'm eighty-nine (if I am lucky enough to live that long), I'll still be able to tackle each day with the same eagerness for discovery and willingness to try something outside my normal lane.

It was just a couple years ago that Mr. Mandelbaum proved he could still do just that. As a lifelong learner, Mr. Mandelbaum is always reading. He reads the law journal every week and keeps himself up to date with whatever developments are happening in the legal field, even though he's already a top professional in his typical areas of practice such as commercial real estate.

One day, Mr. Mandelbaum was at a golf outing with a good friend who was telling him about his girlfriend. She had been harassed and even assaulted over the course of several years by a former employer. It was a classic predator-boss scenario.

At the time of the harassment, the boss was a high-ranking leader in a publicly traded company, so the power differential was sizable. He frequently tried to hit on the woman and constantly wrote her cards and other communications containing inappropriate messages. That happened at a time when those kinds of harassment cases weren't frequently brought, and everyone seemed to get away with it.

By the time the woman came forward with her story, lawyers were telling her the statute of limitations for that kind of claim had expired. She had nothing. However, as Mr. Mandelbaum heard this story from his friend, he remembered having recently read a law journal article that might shed new light on the potential case.

As a result of the sexual abuse involving priests in the Catholic Church, many jurisdictions had begun reopening the books on these kinds of cases, allowing victims of sexual assault to bring cases against past perpetrators, extending the statute of limitations for a certain period of time. This wasn't limited to church clergy, and Mr. Mandelbaum recognized that it might also apply to his friend's girlfriend.

"I don't see why this recent law wouldn't potentially work here," Mandelbaum said. "Tell your girlfriend to reach out to me, and I would be happy to explore this for her."

Mr. Mandelbaum then met the woman, heard her story, and discovered that she had saved all the evidence of her harassment—everything from text messages to notes to cards. Despite what the previous lawyers had told her, he knew she had a case. He agreed to work it on a contingency agreement, which meant she would only pay him if she won a recovery. She had nothing to lose, so she agreed. She was thrilled that someone was willing to help.

Mr. Mandelbaum then sent a letter to her former boss and perpetrator who had since become the CEO of the company where she had worked. Before long, the attorneys for the company reached out to him. Mr. Mandelbaum tactfully and diplomatically explained the facts of the case and asked for a meeting, letting the general counsel know that there was an opportunity to resolve the matter pre-litigation if they took the claim seriously. But he added that the window would not be open forever.

Soon afterward, he got a call from the head employment lawyer at one of the largest law firms in the world. "Your letter has been referred to me for comment," the lawyer said. Mr. Mandelbaum knew he had their attention.

In his classic, old-school style, Mr. Mandelbaum responded, "Rather than us talking about it on the phone or sending emails back and forth, why don't we meet so I can share some evidence you might like to see? Then we can talk about the case."

The lawyer agreed. After seeing the evidence and the case Mr. Mandelbaum had prepared, the lawyer said, "Let me take all this to my client and get back to you." Immediately, the company came back with a very serious offer and promptly negotiated *a multimillion-dollar settlement.*

It was one of the largest fees for a single matter that Mr. Mandelbaum had received in his entire career. Even though he had only worked on the case for a few weeks, through his intelligence, approach, and negotiating savvy, he earned the firm *one million dollars* as the contingency fee. And while the client would have been happy to get any decent recovery for her case, she got to take home approximately *three million dollars.* It was more than she ever imagined.

But none of this would have happened had Mr. Mandelbaum not been a lifelong learner and intellectually curious at heart. It was only because he knew about the new law and how it could apply to this case that he was able to take what would have been kicked to the curb and bring it to new light.

Had Mr. Mandelbaum stayed in his lane, focusing only on his primary area of expertise and not staying abreast of changes in the law, he may have ignored his friend's story and never settled one of the biggest cases of his career. But Mr. Mandelbaum was always open to expanding his horizons and learning something new—and he still is to this day.

When Mr. Mandelbaum initially started in law, the first case he was assigned was a murder case. He defended it, got an acquittal for the defendant, and quickly made a name for himself as a defense lawyer. However, as time went on, he moved from criminal law to matrimonial law to personal injury and commercial litigation. He continued to morph and evolve his areas of focus, eventually becoming one of the most notable commercial real estate lawyers in New Jersey. Even in his late eighties, Mr. Mandelbaum hasn't let that evolution stop. From start to finish, there's no question that lifelong learning has been paramount to his success.

PICKING UP KNOWLEDGE

Whether it was my dad or Mr. Mandelbaum, I've always had mentors who have demonstrated the practical value of developing a wide knowledge base. Another one of my early mentors, Gary Young, used to always remind me how important it is to *know a lot about a lot of things.*

From my own experience, I've seen firsthand that if you have a broad spectrum of knowledge, the number of opportunities that open up for you is exponential.

For example, I consider my legal expertise to be in business, corporate, and transactional law. However, I've always made it my business to know a lot about all other areas of law, which isn't the case for most lawyers. Often, when you ask a corporate lawyer about a matrimonial matter, they won't even want to talk about it. "Let me refer you to so-and-so," they say. "I'm a corporate lawyer. I don't do that."

Instead, I've made it my mission to become familiar with the basics of as many fields as possible. That doesn't mean I've become an expert in every area of law, but it does give me the ability to talk to anyone about any kind of matter a client is confronting, spot the issues, and render some initial advice. As a result, my clients have learned that they can come to me for just about anything. They know I've developed a nose for sniffing out the issues and that I don't just hand them off to someone else because a matter doesn't fall within my typical wheelhouse.

If there's a subject I'm not familiar with, I'm not too proud to bring an expert in, as I often do. However, I always try to go to the meetings and listen in. If there's something I don't understand, I ask questions so I can know how the law works and why the matter needed to be handled in the way it was. I challenge the assumptions and force the attorneys I have brought in to convince me that they have the right plan and vision to handle the matter. If the client is going to believe it is the right path, then I need to believe it too.

As a result, I've learned a lot about any number of areas of law, ranging from litigation to real estate to matrimonial, healthcare, estate and tax planning, elder care, workers' compensation, and personal injury. That way, when a client finds themself confronted with a new legal matter, they know I have a broad knowledge base and can call me first.

Sure, there are always experts who have one niche specialty they can use to bring in business, but by learning *as much as I can* about *everything there is*, I've made myself infinitely more versatile and have expanded my ability to generate business by instilling confidence through sound guidance.

Whether or not you can always see the immediate benefits, being a person in the business of picking up new knowledge consistently pays off.

A MISSION OF GROWTH

I can't claim to be the guy who can replace engines in his driveway like my dad, and I likely don't know quite as much about the law as Mr. Mandelbaum. However, I'd like to think their mission of lifelong learning has rubbed off on me nonetheless. I carry the same aspiration: to continue to learn every day.

One aspect of lifelong learning is never allowing yourself to be satisfied with the status quo. The goal is to always know more, to reach new goals, and to become a better version of yourself. For me, that means being a better leader, a better lawyer, a better advisor, a better boss, a better husband, and a better father. I always want to be better at whatever I set my mind to. I remain painfully aware of it when I fail. But instead of letting that discourage me, I use it as a reminder of why I always want to be better.

To succeed at the mission of continual growth, you need to start with the understanding that you don't know everything. A lot of people act like they're know-it-alls, but the obvious truth is that *no one* really knows it all. There's always room for personal growth and improvement. It's a journey that never ends.

When people ask me how big I want our firm to grow and how many people I want to have, I don't give them a number. I don't believe we can stop growing because the moment we stop growing, we start dying.

Mr. Mandelbaum is a perfect example of that. Of course, health and genetics play a big part in longevity, but there's also something to be said for growing as an antidote to decaying. He hasn't started the dying process because he's not done growing.

If you want to be a lifelong learner, you also have to be willing to make mistakes along the way. When I think about my dad learning how to build houses and fix cars, it's crazy to consider that he never had YouTube to walk him through it. He had to be willing to try different things, figure it out, and make mistakes.

As an enlisted man, Dad didn't have the opportunity to become a pilot when he was in the Air Force, but he didn't let that stop him from learning how to do it when he was nearly fifty years old. "What's the worst that could happen?" he said. "I'll give it a shot." It wasn't long until he got the hang of it, earned his pilot's license, and bought a small plane to take on little trips to nearby states.

Even when he wasn't so successful, Dad didn't let his fear of failure keep him from trying. One thing he tried to learn but never mastered before he died was speaking Japanese. When he was stationed in Japan during his time in the Air Force, he became enamored with Japanese culture. He loved being there and wanted to learn everything there was to know about it. Even after he left the Air Force, when he was in financial printing sales, my father ended up getting the Bank of Japan as a client, which required him to visit Japan once a year.

Dad wanted to be able to master the language so he could engage the culture he so loved. So he practiced, took classes, and even read books on it, but he could never get good at speaking it. He could have let this failure deter him from wanting to continue trying to learn new things, but he never lost sight of his mission of continual evolution.

The world around you is always going to be changing and evolving. So if you don't want to be left behind, you need to evolve. As I think about the entrepreneurs I represent, most of what they do to be successful today isn't the same as what they were doing ten years ago. Likewise, what they'll be doing ten years from now will likely look radically different from what they're currently doing, even if it's in the same business.

If you need an example, just look at artificial intelligence. In the course of just a few years, AI has shifted the way we interact with so many industries. Just like the attorneys who got stuck using dictaphones to transcribe their emails, if you're not willing to continually learn, it won't be long before you become irrelevant and obsolete.

Don't let that be your story. Don't let yourself be satisfied with the status quo. Admit you don't know everything, be willing to take risks, and don't lose sight of your mission of growth.

Around 1960, from Dad's acting portfolio,
always dreaming big dreams

Chapter 4

BET ON YOURSELF

The Leap from Security to Opportunity

A willingness to go out on a limb and bet on yourself is what separates the dreamers from the doers. Especially for people with entrepreneurial vision, an application of this mindset is what makes all the difference. And I can think of no person who better exemplifies this reality than my friend and client Steven D'Angelo.

A number of years back, Steven approached me at a party with a draft of a new business plan. He was excited to talk to me about how he could make it a reality.

"Bill, I want to launch my own gin distillery," he told me. "I want to hear what you think of my business plan."

To say I was surprised would be an understatement.

Wow, that's amazing! I thought. *But is he out of his mind?* On the one hand, I was impressed with Steven's courage to step out on his own and pursue something new and bold. But on the other hand, it seemed like a serious gamble. I had known Steven for a few years. He had a great, secure job on Wall Street. He was making a nice living and was very successful by every metric. What could spur him to take this kind of risk? What did Steven know about launching a distillery?

As I came to find out, he didn't yet know much about the industry, but he was confident in his ability to figure it out. Sure, he had a comfortable position on Wall Street, but he didn't love it, and he didn't see a long-term future in it. Steven was ready to try something new, and he wanted to share that vision with me.

"I'm going to go to Europe for a couple weeks to take this course on learning how to distill gin," he said. "I want to develop a recipe so I can make an artisanal gin product—doing the entire vertical out of New York City, from manufacturing to sales and distribution. I'm going to get a place in the Greenhook section of Brooklyn and call it Greenhook Gin."

In all honesty, I thought it all sounded a little crazy. *I hope he doesn't ask me to invest,* I thought. He didn't, but in retrospect, I sure wish he had. After his trip to Europe, Steven started work on building his business.

It was an audacious undertaking. Micro-breweries had taken off in the 1990s, but the trend had yet to fully expand to gin and spirits. Prior to Steven, only two or three gin distilleries had opened in New York since the Prohibition.

Steven faced a unique set of challenges. Distilling is a highly regulated industry both at the state and federal levels. And in New York, you also have to work with local restrictions. Getting the thing up and running was a considerable feat.

Although he started work on his distillery in 2010, it wasn't until 2012 that he finally launched his brand. At the time, he didn't know the ins and outs of the business, but he believed in himself. One way or another, he was going to get this thing off the ground.

With the help of his family, he eventually brought his product to market, beginning with restaurants and bars—the gatekeepers of the industry—who helped popularize his line of gin, supporting their in-store sales.

At the time, Steven was still pulling double duty—working his job on Wall Street as well as the gin side hustle. He wanted to get a little more proof of concept and still needed to put food on the table in the meantime. But within a few months of the gin's release, a glowing review of Greenhook Gin in *The Wall Street Journal* put Steven on the map. What's more, it gave him the confidence to go all in on himself, and he put in his resignation at his job.

Steven bet on himself, and it paid off in big ways. When the COVID-19 pandemic hit, Steven had the forethought to temporarily convert the distillery to produce hand sanitizer.

For eight weeks, Greenhook made bottles of hand sanitizer until the market caught up to meet the new demand. In that short time, the company earned what it would typically make in three to four years, allowing it to stay afloat through the rest of the pandemic.

Then, in 2022, the company switched directions again, launching a new line of nonalcoholic beverages, including the Phony Negroni and Amaro Falso. That opened Steven up to an entirely new business market that also had the benefit of fewer restrictions. His nonalcoholic drinks took off in no time, and his company launched from being a local brand to one of the fastest-growing nonalcoholic beverage producers in the world.

Everyone has moments when they wonder, *What if I took that risk?* But when Steven was faced with the question, he didn't look primarily at the consequences of potential failure. He thought about the more painful consequences he'd face from living the rest of his life in an unfulfilling job.

At the end of the day, the biggest risk you face isn't failure; it's remaining stuck in something you know will not fulfill you.

THE COST OF PLAYING IT SAFE

From a young age, we're taught that playing it safe is better than taking risks. "Don't rock the boat," they say. "Curiosity killed the cat." "Better safe than sorry." In many ways, this messaging makes sense. Our brains are designed to protect us—to keep us alive by averting any chance of danger. Over time, this instinct has become institutionalized to the point that it's now considered proverbial wisdom.

But what this so-called wisdom often misses is that the costs of playing it safe are just as real—and just as painful—as those we work so hard to avoid. When you choose not to bet on yourself, you block yourself from growth and opportunity. By choosing comfort, you never discover what you're actually capable of doing, and you never reach your full potential. You have *security*, but it comes at the expense of *stagnation*.

When you're stagnant, you're also left feeling stuck. I think about the kind of life Steven D'Angelo would have had if he had never taken the risk to bet on himself. If he had continued his job on Wall Street, which he knew didn't fulfill him, he would have woken up every morning dreading what lay ahead of him. But if he wasn't willing to take the risk, what other choice did he have? He'd have been trapped, stuck in a dead-end job that didn't align with his passion or purpose.

Maybe you can relate. But let me warn you: The longer you wait, the harder it will be to take the leap. In time, you begin to believe that you're too far in. As the years pass you by, you fear the loss of sunk costs if you eventually decide to change. You don't want everything you've invested in so far to become a waste, so you're forced to continue playing it safe.

In the end, all this produces is a life of regret. The nagging voice in the back of your mind taunts you. *What if I had tried? It's too bad I already missed out.* You watch others achieve your dream while you're left watching from the sidelines.

The good news is that this doesn't have to be your story. Another ending is possible *if you have the courage to choose it.*

FROM SECURITY TO OPPORTUNITY

Knowing how and when to bet on yourself is another lesson I learned from my father. His story is one full of risk-taking, but he wasn't taking risks recklessly. In fact, it was quite the opposite.

Dad knew who he was—the kind of person who outworked everyone, overcame setbacks, and never stopped learning. As a result, the leaps he took didn't seem like risks to him at all. He knew that betting on a hard worker like himself was actually the smartest investment he could make.

When I think about the times I saw my dad leap from security to opportunity, one of the first stories that comes to mind is the time he decided to go out on a limb and become a salesman.

It wasn't long after he went back to school and got his degree that he realized if he really wanted to make money in his business, he needed to go into either upper management or sales.

Dad looked at the sales guys and thought, *I've been in customer service. I already know all the people—the lawyers and the investment bankers. I can talk to them. They like me. They know me. They know what I'm all about. Most importantly, they trust me.*

He also could see how far he had already come. Time and again, Dad had overcome obstacles and learned how to do whatever he needed to do to get the job done. If that meant working through the night, he knew he could do it. Based on his own track record of success, he knew his odds were good to bet on himself once again.

So he took the leap. He gave up the security of the management position where he had just gotten comfortable to go into a risky environment based entirely on commission. It was the 1980s, and Dad was in his early fifties. Over the course of the next decade, he worked his way to becoming one of the top salesmen in the industry, eventually making up to $500,000 a year—a pretty high income today but even more so at that time.

But my father's risk-taking didn't end there. Back in 1968, my parents had bought their house for $26,000, and by the time the 1980s rolled around, they had nearly paid it off.

Like most people of their generation, my mom was raised with the idea that the American dream was to work a job, buy a house, pay off your mortgage, and eventually retire in comfort. My dad, however, was born with a little more of an entrepreneurial spirit, and he knew the power of betting on yourself.

While working his job in sales, Dad was also busy studying ways to create wealth outside his typical nine-to-five. After learning a little about real estate and the concept of creating streams of income to support himself in retirement, he decided he wanted to take another leap and invest some money in real estate.

He came home from work one day and took his proposition to my mother. "Hey," he said. "The house is now worth a lot more than when we first got it. We bought it for less than

$30,000, and it's now worth $160,000. Let's take out an equity loan on it and buy an investment property."

My mother must have thought he had lost his mind. They were *this close* to paying off the house, and he wanted to risk it all now by taking on five times the amount of debt of their first mortgage. She was on the verge of tears. To her, that seemed like the craziest thing he could do.

But Dad believed in his own ability to figure things out and make it happen. *I'll find something at the right price*, he thought. *I'll renovate it myself, and I'll watch as it appreciates in value. I'll do all the work needed to rent it out and make it successful.*

And that he did. In the years to come, my father worked his way up to owning and renting out nearly a dozen properties. And by making clever use of a provision in the tax code that allowed for their accelerated depreciation, he was able to get tax write-offs that made his personal income—about half a million dollars—essentially tax-free.

Dad eventually sold most of those properties when the 1986 tax law took away accelerated depreciation, but he used the profits to build a new apartment building and buy additional commercial rental properties. As I sit here today, my siblings and I still own those properties, which are now debt-free and fully rented. After my dad passed away, they served as a reliable form of income for my mom. Today, their value is likely in the millions.

In the end, Dad's vision paid off. It was a big risk to take on all that debt at his age. He gambled the security he and my mom had worked so hard to secure. In his mind, however, there wasn't anything that wouldn't work for him if he learned enough about it and put his mind to it.

AVOIDING REGRET

Throughout my life, my dad's example of taking calculated risks has stuck with me. It has also helped prepare me for the day I was faced with a choice of my own—a choice of either sticking with security or stepping out in search of something far more meaningful.

After graduating from law school at the University of Virginia, I started my career working at what was then the third-largest law firm in the world. From an outside perspective, I was living the dream. I was working in New York City and had the highest compensation you can get as an inexperienced new lawyer. That kind of lucrative job was especially desirable for a young professional looking to get out from under his student loans.

Although my dream had always been to be a big Wall Street lawyer, I quickly realized that my work was missing a crucial element: *I wanted to help people.*

For as long as I can remember, being a hero to others has been a core part of how I see myself. I want to help change others' lives in a meaningful way, work with them one-on-one, and see the real purpose behind what I do. But that wasn't a feeling I got slaving away for a mid-level vice president at some international corporation, working to ensure he could still get his annual bonus.

The corporation had me working every night and every weekend. I remember one time on Easter Sunday, a car was waiting outside my house so they could haul me back to the office the moment dinner was finished. Why? I was working on a potential sale for the New York Mets, and there was a due diligence book that had to be completed by the next day.

The job demanded total devotion. Every deadline was immediate. Every task was an all-nighter. And despite all the hard work the staff put in, we were all just hoping we wouldn't be the person on the chopping block when layoffs came.

I didn't like the feeling of being a cog in someone else's machine. Working in that kind of environment was not sustainable. It was horrible—like working in a sweatshop—an existence that was totally incompatible with having any life of my own and so contrary to my entrepreneurial spirit.

The moment of choice came one night as I stood in my apartment and looked at my face in the mirror. I was in my late twenties, yet I had dark circles around my eyes. I looked like I had been hit by a bus, and I felt like it too. I was completely exhausted. I was in a city of millions, yet it felt like I was totally alone. *Oh my gosh,* I thought. The place has sucked the life out of me. How could I even be standing at that point?

As I thought about the partners who stayed in my department long term, I realized that not one of them was happy. In fact, every partner in the department had been divorced at least once. There were no exceptions. Not one of them had a successful marriage. How could they? If they were never home, they didn't have any time to invest in their relationships.

Any marriage is hard work. That's why the national divorce rate is around 50 percent. But I at least wanted to stack the deck in my favor, and a 0 percent batting average did not sound promising to me. I wanted to be both physically and mentally present with my family rather than being one of those guys who pats himself on his back for going to one of their kids' games occasionally.

As I thought about what I wanted to do, I remember getting advice from my dad. "Billy," he said. "If there's a time in your life you're going to make a bold move, do it now because right now you have the ability to do it. As time goes on, you're going to get bumps in your salary each year, and you're going to continue to adjust to a more expensive lifestyle. After a few years, you'll become a white elephant, having tied yourself down to one specialty. You'll feel like you have no other choice but to continue where you are if you want to maintain your lifestyle. So if you're going to make a leap, do it now."

His advice really resonated with me. If I were going to cut my income in half by going somewhere else, it made sense to do it then rather than later. So I left my 1,200-lawyer firm to go where I would be lawyer number twenty-one.

My friends thought I was out of my mind. "Are you crazy?" they asked me. "You have one of the best jobs you can get as a lawyer, and you're going to give it all up?" They thought I was already at the pinnacle, but I knew it wasn't for me.

I was ready for a new opportunity—one that would let me come into myself as an entrepreneurial lawyer, build my own clientele, and develop meaningful relationships with my clients. I was ready not to rely on anyone and make my own assignments from the clients I got myself.

By my second year at the new firm and because I was able to earn based on commission, I was making as much as the colleagues I had left behind at the big firm in New York. But more importantly, I was doing purposeful work. I was enjoying my life, and I felt the joy of building something that was genuinely helping other people.

Twenty-six years later, my name is on the side of the building, I've raised a wonderful family, and I am doing work that I love. The firm has grown exponentially, and we now employ over 120 lawyers and 230 employees, and we're growing. That decision I made back in my twenties turned out to be one of the most fundamental, life-changing moments for me. It shaped the trajectory of my life. I bet on myself, and there's no denying it was well worth the risk.

REFRAMING RISK

If you ask any successful entrepreneur, they'll tell you the key to success isn't learning how to avoid risk at all costs. It's learning how and when to bet on yourself with confidence.

Often, the biggest hurdle to betting on yourself is the misguided belief that playing it safe always pans out better in the long run. However, even a basic understanding of finances shows that this isn't true. If all you did was play it safe, you'd never invest your money in anything. You'd hide it under your mattress or let it all sit in a savings account earning mere pennies of interest instead of using it to its full potential to earn you exponentially more.

Those who are most financially successful know that calculated risk is often worth it. When you know what you're investing in, you can trust with greater certainty that it will eventually produce a reliable return.

The same is true with betting on yourself. You're not going in blind. You know what kind of person you are and what you're capable of. If you know you're a person who will outwork everyone, overcome setbacks, and never stop learning, you can reframe betting on yourself as a calculated investment instead of a risky gamble.

Remember, the greatest risk comes from always playing it safe, and the cost of stagnation, unfulfillment, and regret is too high a price to pay. *By choosing purpose over comfort, you can create the life you want for yourself.*

Early 2000s, annual fishing trip to Canada
with Dad's friend/client, Joe Trinkle

Chapter 5

MAKE BUSINESS PERSONAL

The Importance of Relationships

If you've ever worked with someone who sees you as nothing more than a line item on a spreadsheet, you understand what it feels like to be in a transactional relationship. It's cold. It's distant. It only lasts as long as the matter, assignment, or contract requires and not a moment more.

Thankfully, that's not how Dad operated. When it came to work and life, he didn't divide people into two different classes of relationships. He simply treated everyone like they mattered.

Why? Because to him, *they did.*

Business wasn't about squeezing every last dollar out of a deal. It was about creating a real, human connection and showing up when it really counted.

When my father left his large, global printing company to join a much smaller, regional company, the transition wasn't easy. Many of his previous clients had resorted to using other companies for their printing needs during his transition time, and it was hard for him to win many of them back. Dad's new firm didn't have the same brand-name recognition or resources that made them competitive for big bids. Clients who were accustomed to a certain level of polish were now being asked to take a chance on a small business that was still finding its footing—a risk some of them were not willing to take. As he recounted, that was when the real, personal relationships he had built over the years truly came through for him.

One such relationship was with a man named Joe Trinkle. Joe was an executive at AT&T and had been a loyal client of my dad's for many years. But Joe wasn't just a client; he was a *friend.* What began as a business relationship had grown much deeper. Over the years, Joe and my father had gone on numerous fishing trips together. Our families knew each other and invited one another to family parties and events. And when Dad was forced to start his business again from ground zero, that friendship held.

Joe's loyalty meant everything to Dad. Normally, big companies whose printing budgets were measured in *truckloads* of paper wouldn't go to small businesses like my father's for their needs. But because Dad had always gone above and beyond for Joe, Joe was willing to put his neck on the line for my dad when it mattered most.

There was one night in particular that my dad always talked about. He and Joe were working late on a financial prospectus in my father's new office. Gone were the perks of the big firm—the large luxurious offices, fancy catered meals, and endless support staff. Now it was just a small crew staying late in a modest Midtown building trying to hit a deadline.

It was well after midnight when they finally wrapped up. The team was tired and ready to head home, but then they realized the elevators had shut down. *The building wasn't open twenty-four hours, and security had left for the night.*

Their only option was to use the service elevator, which had not been locked down for the night. So there they were— Dad, Joe Trinkle, and a few corporate lawyers—crammed into a service elevator full of smelly garbage bags from the cleaning crew.

Most people would have turned up their noses, questioning why they were doing business in a place like that. But Joe just laughed. He turned to my dad and jokingly said, "Dave, you're building this business from the ground up, and I'll ride with you anywhere—even in the garbage elevator."

That line always stuck with me. Joe had every reason to walk away and say, "I really love Dave, but this is a big ask." My dad no longer had the support of a big company. He didn't have the same resources. Joe could have taken his business anywhere. But Joe didn't care about any of that. He stayed because the relationship was real.

And Joe wasn't the only one. There was also Rhoda Andrews, another longtime client who stuck by my dad through thick and thin. Rhoda was in charge of the annual proxy statement and notice to shareholders for Lucent Technologies. It was a job that required printing millions of copies—literal tractor-trailers full of paper. The scale was enormous, and so was the expense.

For a company like my dad's to even bid on such a huge job—let alone win it—was shocking. But because of his established relationship with Rhoda, she went out on a limb for him, and he was awarded the project.

Rhoda was under constant pressure from her bosses to cut costs wherever possible, especially given the enormous size of this project. However, my dad's income for the project was commission-based. The bigger the job was, the bigger the payout for him.

To help Rhoda cut costs meant going against his personal interests as her provider, but my dad didn't see it that way. For him, it was more about doing the right thing and helping a friend look good rather than protecting his bottom line.

During one of these yearly bids, Dad had just undergone surgery for cancer and was getting chemo. It was a rough recovery, and his doctors had ordered him to rest and not work for a period of time. However, the Lucent Annual Report job was going to press, and he couldn't leave Rhoda and her team without support, especially because of everything she'd done for him. So when Rhoda was trying to find ways to cut costs, my dad got creative instead of telling her that her problem wasn't his. He started brainstorming solutions and came up with an idea: *Why don't they make the report smaller than the traditional size?* He worked with the designers, pitched a half-size booklet to Lucent, and helped Rhoda get SEC approval for the novel change.

Instead of following the doctor's orders, Dad ended up living out of a hotel for a week while he worked through long days and late nights with the clients to get the job done. He cared too much about doing a great job for Rhoda and Lucent to let someone else see it through.

In the end, it saved the company a fortune. But it also meant he made less money on that job. However, prioritizing his relationship paid off in the long run. He kept the Lucent account for several years, right up until the company ceased to exist. Why? Because when you prioritize the personal relationship and do what's right for the client, the business tends to follow.

However, he didn't do it with the business in mind. He helped other people because he genuinely cared about them. It was the *relationships* and being a hero to others that gave him personal joy and a fulfilling life.

That care was evident in the way he stayed with people, even when they couldn't be of financial benefit to him anymore. As Greg Peck, the general counsel of Corning Glass, told me, "Your father was one of the only people who became my actual friend in business."

That was the key. Dad wasn't trying to turn clients into lifelong customers. He was just being a friend. That friendship is what pushed him to stay late, answer the calls, and take the long drives. It's why he showed up when it mattered—and because he did, those people stayed with him in return, even when it meant riding in a garbage elevator in the middle of the night.

Those relationships weren't built on contracts. They were built on trust.

However, not everyone does business that way. Some people draw hard lines between business and personal. They see personal relationships as a conflict or complication and falsely believe that professionalism demands distance.

That kind of approach might work for a while. After all, anyone can do business when everything is going well. But when things inevitably go wrong, those thin relationships don't hold up. That's when the loyalty that only comes from real relationships makes all the difference.

THE MYTH OF THE WORK-LIFE DIVIDE

Unfortunately, few people are willing to do business the way my dad did. Not everyone wants to make it personal. In fact, there's a whole school of thought out there that says you shouldn't. They tell you that business is business, that personal is personal, and that you shouldn't blur the lines. The goal is to have a work-life balance where you divvy up your life into separate categories that never overlap.

On the surface, that might sound reasonable. If you can completely detach your work life from the rest of your life, you might be able to make space to enjoy your life a little more. But from my experience, when you keep business purely transactional, it's a mistake. Work becomes a drain for you and everyone else you come in contact with.

I've worked with clients who see every interaction as a means to an end, and you can always tell it right away. There's no hiding it. They never ask how you're doing and don't remember your kids' names. They don't care what's going on in your life, and they definitely don't want to hear about it. They only care about results, and if you can't provide them in the way they want, they'll find someone else who will. You're not a real person to them, just a human vending machine.

Those kinds of clients never last. When there's no real relationship, you're only as good as what you can deliver. There's no goodwill, margin for error, or sense of trust. And as soon as a better deal is on the table, they're gone, and they aren't looking back.

Clearly, those aren't the kind of clients you want. As an entrepreneur, there's no way you can build a lasting business on that kind of foundation. The constant pressure to perform perfectly or get replaced would be exhausting and unsustainable.

When you only have transactional relationships, the emotional toll from that kind of dynamic is real. You see their name come up on your phone, and you feel a jolt of dread. You already know that the call is going to be demanding, impersonal, and probably thankless. Of course, because you're a professional, you still take the call and execute accordingly. But your heart's not in it. It doesn't make you want to go the extra mile because when people don't care about you, it's hard to be passionate about the work.

Beyond that, when business isn't personal, it becomes incredibly fragile. That's because purely transactional relationships don't hold up when pressure hits. There's no loyalty or helping hand when you're in need. When the time comes that you need help, their question will be "What have you done for me lately?"

Impersonal business also comes with a deeper, unseen cost—one most people don't think about until it's too late. When you make business transactional, you don't just lose out on loyalty. You lose opportunities for new connections too.

Some of the best clients I've ever had didn't start with business deals. They started with conversations. By making myself available to others and leading with relationships, they learned they could trust me. Then, when a business need did come up, they felt like they could come to me.

That was certainly the case with Ralph DeMayo, the owner of Mountain Deli. Back when I was a second-year lawyer, I used to stop in there nearly every day to grab a sandwich. As Ralph prepared it (freshly sliced every time, of course), we chatted about everything from family to sports to weekend plans, day after day.

Over time, we built a real friendship—right there in the deli. Then the day came when Ralph asked me for my card.

He said he wanted to call me after work because he needed help setting up a business entity his CPA had recommended. I followed up, and Ralph introduced me to that CPA, a gentleman named Howard Bielski.

That introduction changed everything. Howard and I began working in conjunction with each other. Over time, we exchanged dozens of clients. We've been through the highs and lows of life together—weddings, losses of loved ones, and family milestones. To this day, Howard is still my personal accountant and one of my closest friends.

All that came from a series of genuine conversations over the sandwich counter. There was no plan or angle, just a real, human connection that led to a series of open doors.

That doesn't happen when you treat relationships transactionally. When you treat people merely as machines, they're not as likely to give you referrals. Referrals happen when people see you as someone who genuinely cares and is worthy of their trust. When you keep people at arm's length, you're only hurting yourself.

This isn't just true for clients either. It's also the case for your coworkers, your employees, and your team. When you don't take the time to really get to know the people you work with, you miss out on culture, camaraderie, and the feeling of pulling together toward something bigger than a paycheck. Frankly, you miss out on the fun of collaboration, working together, and enjoying each other's company in the process.

Instead, you get into your silos. It's everyone for themselves. Instead of watching out for each other, your team learns to only watch out for themselves. The result? Your team becomes fragile. As soon as there's a bump in the road—a deal falls apart, the market tanks, and the business takes a hit—those people don't rally. They look for the exit. That's the price of building a work-life barrier.

People don't stay for money alone. They stick around when they like, respect, and enjoy the people they work with. The deeper the bonds are within your organization, the more stickiness you create in terms of retention. Trust me, as long as the compensation is fair, culture and deep relationships beat money every time.

When you never let anyone behind the relational wall, the job eventually stops being rewarding. It becomes a grind— hours to fill and money to chase. You can't wait to get off the clock and make it to the weekend. Finally, you start to lose sight of why you started in the first place.

Even if you do manage to achieve business success with that kind of setup, the payoff loses its luster, and you're left with nothing—no real connections that will outlast the work.

At the end of the day, it's your choice. You can choose to keep your work buttoned up and at arm's length, but if you ask me, it's no real way to live.

RELATIONSHIPS WITH RESILIENCE

We often don't acknowledge how valuable things are until we fear they may be gone. That was certainly the case for me when in March 2020 I came to fully appreciate the value of personal relationships in the workplace.

One day the firm and I were operating at full speed—attending meetings, traveling, and taking clients out to business dinners. The next thing I knew, the COVID-19 pandemic hit, and the world came to an abrupt halt. All the momentum we'd built was suddenly gone.

There were no more networking events and no more water-cooler conversations. I didn't have the choice of face-to-face relationship-building. Work became sitting at a quiet desk at home, looking at a calendar that had never appeared so empty.

Like everyone else at the time, I felt a gnawing sense of uncertainty. *What now? How do you keep a business alive when you can't do the things that built it in the first place?*

But then something unexpected happened. Coworkers and clients started calling me. It wasn't because they had a deal on the table or a contract to review. In fact, they weren't calling to ask for anything. They called to check in. They wanted to see how I was doing, how my family was, and what it felt like being home all day. And they shared their experiences and perspectives too.

I started doing the same. I found myself scrolling through old contacts—people who may have begun as clients but who quickly became friends through work. I'd see a name and think, *I wonder how he's holding up. I should reach out.*

What came out of those conversations was *everything*. I didn't realize it at the time, but all those years of truly showing up for people had planted something—seeds of trust, friendship, and genuine connection. When everything else was stripped away, those were the people I gravitated to—the same people who gravitated to me as well.

You wouldn't believe it, but that year ended up being the most successful of my entire career thus far. It wasn't because I found some secret formula for conducting the best Zoom calls or because I launched a brilliant marketing campaign. It was because of the *relationships* that had been established long before the crisis ever hit.

The pandemic proved that these relationships weren't mere transactional connections. These were people I had shared meals with, laughed with, and stayed late for. As a result, they were people who called just to catch up. They were people I had celebrated with when things were going great, and they became people who stood by when things seemed dire.

Those bonds didn't just hold; *they got stronger.* COVID-19 showed me that when things get hard, people don't reach for the cheapest option. *They reach for the most trusted one.* They reach for someone they know will stand with them in the storm. However, if you never put in the effort to make the relationship personal, they'll never be able to trust that you will.

Seeing the depth of these relationships reminded me so much of my father. He built his business on genuine connection. And because he was real and reliable, he built an unbreakable bond of loyalty.

That kind of loyalty doesn't show up on your profit and loss statements. It doesn't live in the analytics report. But it is the single greatest reason people come back to you, refer others to you, and stick by your side when things get tough.

When the pandemic stripped away all the structure, what was left were the relationships. Everything else went away, but the people didn't disappear. They showed up stronger than ever.

That experience reminded me that blurring the line between friend and colleague isn't something to fear. In fact, it can be your greatest asset.

Relationships aren't just good *for* business. They *are* the business. For your business to thrive, it all starts by making it personal.

YOU'LL ENJOY

Most of our waking hours are spent on the job and at work. Love it or hate it—it's just the math. Considered this way, the choice should be obvious: *Why wouldn't you want to make that time as meaningful, fulfilling, and enjoyable as possible?*

Ultimately, that's what making business personal is all about. At its core, it's not about networking, expanding your reach, or getting more referrals—though those things can and often do happen along the way. Making business personal is really about building a working life that actually feels like a life you enjoy.

Imagine what it would be like if 90 percent of the people you work with—whether coworkers or clients—were people you considered friends. I don't just mean people you tolerate or have learned to deal with. I mean people you really like and respect, the kind of people you'd want to get drinks with. How much lighter would your days be if that were your reality?

That's the benefit that people often miss when they approach work and life with the goal of keeping them separate—business over here and personal life over there. They don't realize how much better the whole experience of work can be when the people who are involved in it actually matter to them.

When business becomes personal, you're no longer just grinding to get through. You're showing up for people you want to help. You become excited to celebrate their wins, and you don't feel a sense of dread when you see them calling. You look forward to meetings because you know they'll come with real conversations between friends. Every day you come into the office, you're sharing ideas and solving problems with the same people you'd want to spend time with on the weekends. That's a different kind of workday—and it makes a different kind of life.

When I think about the people I work most closely with today, they're overwhelmingly people I like being around. That didn't happen by accident. It happened because I never tried to keep things sterile. Following the example my dad set for me, I've allowed the personal side of who I am to come through in my work. I ask people about their lives. I follow up. I stay curious. I let relationships grow—not as a means to an end but because I want to have a work life that's worth living.

When you build real relationships into the fabric of your business, work goes from being a drain to something that's actually energizing. You look at your calendar and find yourself looking forward to the calls on it. You think, *Yeah, that's going to be a good conversation. That's someone I can't wait to talk to.* And when enough of your calendar is filled with people like that, everything changes.

That doesn't mean the hard stuff goes away. You'll still have tough conversations and weeks where everything hits at once. But when those moments do come, they'll happen in the context of strong, reliable relationships. It won't be you against the world because you'll be able to trust that your team will be pulling alongside you.

What I've also learned is that relationships affect your endurance. When you feel connected to the people you're working with, you stop burning out as quickly. You're not just exchanging time for money. You're spending time with people who bring out your best and fill your tank in a real way. When you make business personal, you create a work life that's worth living and that's capable of keeping you going.

But how do you do that practically?

I've spoken with a lot of young professionals over the years—people trying to figure out how much of themselves they ought to bring to work. They want to do it right—balancing the personal and professional—but they're not sure what that actually looks like in practice. What I always tell them is this: *Be real. Be consistent. Be someone you'd want to work with.*

That doesn't mean you need to be the life of the party. You don't have to be an extrovert or the loudest voice in the room, but it does mean you have to care. You have to genuinely care about the person sitting across from you and communicate that care in a real way.

Genuine care is something you can't fake. Be reliable. Be thoughtful. Say what you mean, and follow through. Help when you can, even if there's nothing in it for you. Most importantly, be intentional about getting to know the people you're working with as real people.

When you do, you build relationships that are durable and that are capable of weathering life's storms. By making business personal, you can build a career worth doing.

In the end, you're not just building a business; you're building your life. Life doesn't pause when you walk through the front doors of your office building, so don't treat it that way.

You can choose to go into work every day with people you consider friends—helping people you genuinely like, and being yourself along the way. So why wouldn't you?

Dad (second from left) competing in NY State Open
Spearfishing Tournament at almost sixty years old

Chapter 6

DEVELOP AN ABUNDANCE MINDSET

The Key to Transformative Relationships

When you approach relationships believing that there's more than enough to go around, you free yourself from the burden of obsessing over your own interests. And you enable yourself to think about the needs of others. Operating out of an abundance mindset helps you be a hero to other people, creating transformative relationships they don't soon forget.

All his life, my father showed me what it means to live from abundance, regardless of whether he actually had a lot. He made it his practice to help others and celebrate them in their successes, even when doing so seemed to go against his own interests.

When my dad worked in sales at his financial printing company, he devoted much of his time to mentoring younger salespeople who were just trying to make their way. Helping them didn't provide a direct benefit to him. In fact, any client he helped a newcomer secure meant one more client who didn't go to him. But Dad didn't look at it that way. He got a unique sense of joy out of helping others, and that alone made it worth it.

By looking out for other people, even when it didn't directly benefit him, my father left a lasting impression. When he passed away, I heard story upon story from people he helped along the way. One such individual was my tee-ball coach, Mr. McGotty.

As I stood in the receiving line at my father's funeral, greeting people who'd come to pay their respects, I was surprised to see Mr. McGotty and his wife in the line. *That's really nice of them to come,* I thought. They knew Dad from having been part of the same small lake community and through youth sports, but they didn't really know him that well.

However, as they got closer to the front, I realized that they both had tears in their eyes. *What's going on?* I thought. *There's got to be more to the story.* When the McGottys finally got to the front, they shared with me how, back when Mr. McGotty was my tee-ball coach, my dad had helped them out in a big way when they needed it most.

Nearly thirty years earlier, Mr. McGotty had lost his job and was going through a tough time. My father, who was working as a customer service manager at the time, helped create a job for Mr. McGotty as a messenger, helping out where needed so he could get on the payroll at the printing company.

"If it had not been for your father, we could have lost our house. He didn't have to, but he went out of his way to help us. We'll always be so grateful for what he did for us."

As I stood there listening to their story, I started to get choked up. I had no idea my father had done all that—but it shouldn't have surprised me. That was just the kind of person he was. He believed that success could be shared, and he lived his life committed to helping others.

As humans, scarcity is our default setting, *but it doesn't have to be*. Regardless of your current level of success, you can choose to operate out of an abundance mindset.

You can choose to believe in a bigger, brighter, better future.

You can choose to believe that collaboration is greater than competition.

And you can choose to believe that others' success doesn't mean your failure.

When you do, you set yourself up for a life that you'll actually enjoy—one that's marked by transformative relationships rather than merely transactional ones.

THE THREAT OF SCARCITY

Far too often, people fall into the trap of believing that success in life is a zero-sum game. They think that if someone else wins, it means *they lose*. As a result, when they see others succeeding, they feel threatened rather than inspired by it.

I see it everywhere, even with people working on Wall Street who are making millions a year. Of all people, they should feel successful, right? But because someone across the hall is making just a little bit more, it ruins it for them. They feel like they're behind, that they don't have enough.

Why? *Because they're stuck in a scarcity mindset.* For people who think that way, comparison becomes a deadly trap. It robs them of their happiness and makes them hoard what they have in a desperate attempt to feel secure. It incentivizes thinking only about themself, making them reluctant to share or give what they have to others. In the end, it can make them ruthless, leaving them with a stained reputation that will follow them everywhere they go.

Several years ago, I was in Las Vegas for a big convention. I was sitting at a dinner table when one of my friends pointed out an individual who was walking by.

"Bill," he said. "There goes Brandon."

Woah, I thought, immediately recognizing the name. Brandon was a managing partner of a major law firm working in the same space as we were. In some ways, the firm was a competitor to us. However, it was even bigger than ours, and I was always impressed with what Brandon had accomplished.

He had built a successful, nationwide firm, and I was eager to meet him.

"Have you met Brandon before?" my friend asked.

"No, but I'd love to," I quickly answered.

"I'm shocked you guys have never met. I know him well," he said. "Let me introduce you."

A few minutes later, Brandon was walking back near our table, and my friend flagged him down. "Hey, Brandon! Let me introduce you to my good friend Bill Barrett."

"Hi, I'm Bill," I said. "I am the CEO at Mandelbaum Barrett. It's great to meet you."

I watched as Brandon instinctively took a step back.

He shot me a bizarre look and said, "Record f*ing revenue, bro. Record f*ing revenue." And with that, he walked off.

I was blown away. *What just happened? Did he really just do that?* Apparently, I had somehow made it onto Brandon's radar as a growing firm that had been gaining momentum in that industry. And to him, that alone made me not just his competition but his enemy.

That wasn't how I approached the situation *at all.* In my mind, I was hoping to become friends with the guy—a friendly competitor even. I would have loved the opportunity to get to know Brandon, develop a professional rapport, and become friends and colleagues. I'd have liked to get a meal, hear about all the things he had done, and learn from someone who had already climbed the mountain.

Coming from a place of abundance, this meeting seemed like a real opportunity to me. Brandon and I could have compared notes, referred to each other clients and transactions whenever we had conflicts of interest, or even done joint seminars together. I believed we were capable of much more together than we would be able to achieve apart.

However, since he seemed to be coming from a place of scarcity, our meeting was anything but that. He viewed me as a competitor—an adversary. For him to win at the level he wanted, I needed to lose. End of story.

I've since heard other stories about Brandon that further support this theory. And what is the consequence of this scarcity mindset? Brandon has blocked himself off from developing transformative relationships—the kind of real relationships built on mutual trust and commitment that offer growth and development. Instead, by keeping his focus only on his own needs—building a fat pocketbook instead of a reputation of respect—he's created a purely transactional world that will last only as long as the money flows.

LEADING WITH YOUR GIVING HAND

Working in the same lane as someone else doesn't mean you have to be their enemy. In fact, when you lead with your giving hand rather than with a clenched fist, you'll discover unexpected benefits that you'd never have realized alone.

Leading with an abundance mindset was first modeled to me by my father, but it's only been further ingrained throughout my career. When I was coming up as a young attorney, my mentor, Mr. Mandelbaum, was by far the top revenue earner in our firm. Over the years, I began inching my way closer to having a book of business at his level.

One day, another attorney at the firm told me, "You know, Bill, he's never going to let you earn more money than him."

That comment struck me. *Why would he say that?* I thought. *I know Mr. Mandelbaum pretty well, and I really believe that if I earned it, he'd be the first to congratulate me on making more money. Not unlike Dad, Mr. Mandelbaum would be the happiest guy in the world on my behalf.*

What I knew that this attorney didn't was that Barry Mandelbaum didn't get where he was by operating under a scarcity mindset. He wasn't threatened by me at all—or anyone else, for that matter. In fact, Mr. Mandelbaum loved seeing other people succeed—especially the people closest to him. Seeing others succeed always gave him joy. He nurtured people, developed them, and tried to make everyone around him more successful. So I knew Mr. Mandelbaum would be my biggest cheerleader and supporter.

As it turned out, I was right. When we reached the year's end and saw that my performance and efforts on behalf of the firm had risen to the level where I deserved to earn more, Mr. Mandelbaum was thrilled. He told me how proud he was of my accomplishment and that he hoped others would soon follow. He said that was what the firm needed to thrive in future generations. *Why?* Because he believed that a rising tide really does lift all boats. His legacy is the building of an institution that not only has already provided for generations but, more importantly, is one that will provide for generations to come.

Now I have the opportunity to help others in the same way Mr. Mandelbaum helped me. As CEO of Mandelbaum Barrett, I love collaborating with other attorneys at our firm. I'm happy to share my business with them or even give them complete access to my long-term clients to let them develop direct personal relationships. I'm thrilled when people create new opportunities or bring in new clients, and I don't feel threatened by the idea of others surpassing me. Their success is success for me and the firm, and it's what's needed to continue this special and unique firm for future generations.

When you operate out of abundance, you realize that you're not really in competition with other people; you're just in competition with *yourself*. Your goal is to always be beating your own records, just as you want others to be beating theirs. Abundance makes you excited to see success in all its forms, wherever it may be—even when it's for the so-called competition.

This past year, hockey player Alex Ovechkin of the Washington Capitals broke Wayne Gretzky's career record for the most goals ever scored in professional hockey. Following this achievement, Gretzky personally congratulated Ovechkin on the new record. He did it with grace and humility and consistently talked about how wonderful it was for the game of hockey. That's abundance.

In my region, there's a young lawyer named Paul who has been in the process of building his own firm that targets some of the same primary markets as ours. I've watched him make new headway year over year, adding new employees and growing his firm's reach. And even though he's considered a direct competitor, I've loved seeing him succeed over time and have enjoyed watching his continued growth and success.

As Paul began learning the tricks of the trade, he reached out to me and my partner to pick our brains about growing and building a firm. We compared notes about what we were seeing in the market. And because I've made it my practice to operate out of abundance rather than scarcity, our firm developed a transformational relationship with Paul.

Over the years, we've gone out to lunch to "talk shop" about business, clients, and growth. We have always been an open book, and so has he. It's my hope that we gave Paul the experience I wish I'd had when I met Brandon at that conference many years before in Las Vegas.

Over the years, Paul's firm and mine have referred several clients to each other. Whenever my firm has had a conflict of interest, we've sent clients Paul's way, and he's done the same with us. Paul has also sent us clients who require specific expertise that falls outside the scope of what his firm can handle.

When you live out of an abundance mindset, you will always be surprised how it eventually comes back to you. When you lead with your giving hand, people want to give back. It's human nature. We want to be around people who see the world this way. Whether in business or in our personal lives, we're drawn to people who freely give what they have, trusting that there's more than enough to go around.

You get to choose what kind of relationships you'll have. Do you want to be like Brandon who sees his peers as enemies and develops a reputation for being ruthless? Or do you want the kind of relationships that celebrate success and lift all boats?

COLLABORATION OVER COMPETITION

The key to overcoming scarcity and living in abundance starts with getting past the idea that it's winners versus losers. In every level of business, there are always people who think that someone else's success inherently means their loss. They act as if an open door for someone else is the same as a closed door for them.

But the way I was raised, that couldn't be any further from the truth. The reality is that you don't have to live in a self-preserving silo. You don't have to be so proprietary about your opportunities. Our primitive instincts lead us to hoard for ourselves, but life doesn't have to be a zero-sum, winner-takes-all game. Rooting for others and wanting other people to be successful doesn't mean you have to be left with the crumbs.

It doesn't have to be winners versus losers.

To clarify, that certainly doesn't mean you should lie down and let other people walk all over you. Of course, you should still be invested in your own success, but the necessary shift in thinking is that your success isn't defined by others' losses.

For example, whenever I'm negotiating an agreement on behalf of one of my clients, I always begin by asking myself, *What's important to my client? What do they need in this situation?* Then, my goal in the negotiation is to ensure my client's interests are protected.

The potential danger comes when you approach a negotiation thinking it's about winning a fight rather than ensuring your needs are met. With that mentality, your goals can quickly shift from protecting your client's interests to making sure the person on the other side doesn't get theirs. Scarcity tempts you to use whatever leverage you have to take everything the other side wants—to pound them to oblivion without reason even when it's not necessary in order to get your client what they need.

Unfortunately, there are many people in my profession who seek to do just that, and they're the reason the legal profession often has such a bad reputation. They think that pushing other people down is the best way to lift themselves up. What they don't realize is that they're missing out on transformative relationships and hurting their client services as a result.

When you intentionally push others down and view everyone as your competition, nobody wants to be around you. They might be friendly with you when they think they can get something out of you, but deep down, they don't really like you at all. The moment you're no longer useful to them, they're done with you. There's no loyalty and no long-term benefit because the relationship is purely transactional.

However, when you live out of abundance, you become the kind of person others want to be around. You're confident, generous, and eager to support other people. You're capable of having real, transformative relationships with people. You don't treat others like they're disposable, and they're eager to support you in return.

I've seen this pattern time and again in my own life. Because I'm not needlessly combative when I'm at the negotiation table, I leave the door open for positive relationships with my peers.

In one instance, I had just finished settling a matter with another attorney. "Hey," I told him. "We did some really great work together for our clients and kept them out of litigation. I'd love to take you out to lunch to celebrate the good work we did for our clients."

He was genuinely surprised. We had just gone through a negotiation on opposite sides of the table, so it might have been natural for him to assume that I thought of him as my adversary. Most attorneys would.

Nevertheless, he agreed to get together the next Friday after work to toast our accomplishments. At the time, I didn't think anything of it. After all, I was operating out of an abundance mindset, and I was eager to celebrate both our wins.

The Monday after our Friday get-together—literally three days later—I found out that my small gesture had paid off in big ways. The attorney called me, along with his managing partner. As it turned out, they had a very significant client they would no longer be able to represent.

"We have this hopeless conflict of interest," they told me. "We've had this client and their entire family with us for a while, but now there's a dispute between two of the owners of the company. We've represented all the owners' family members at one time or another, so there's no way we can handle this case. We are likely going to lose the relationship completely. However, one of the owners still thinks enough of us and our years of guidance that he has asked us for a recommendation. We suggested they call you."

I couldn't believe it. When I offered to get lunch with that attorney, I had no agenda and no idea I would get something in return. I just thought, *This attorney was a nice guy and a good lawyer. Why not try to be friends?*

But you never know what's going to come back your way. The next thing I knew, the client interviewed me and hired me to handle their sensitive family dispute. The matter ended up producing hundreds of thousands of dollars in legal fees and finished with a very favorable outcome for the client. But that was only the start. After that case concluded, I asked the owner of the company if I could bring my team in to present all the other things we could do for them. One thing led to another, and we ended up retaining that company as a long-term client. Over the next few years, we further developed our business relationship and consistently did over a million dollars a year in legal work for them.

Who would have guessed that my so-called adversary would connect me to one of the biggest clients in my career? But because I never viewed him as my adversary, that possibility became reality.

Coaching the middle school varsity girls soccer team

Chapter 7

SHARE YOUR TIME

The Measure of True Generosity

When I first began working in New York City between college and law school, I had to catch the early bus out of New Jersey to get to work each morning. The Lakeland bus took me from the suburbs west of New York City to the Port Authority bus terminal. On a good day, the ride was one hour. On a bad day, it could be two or even three hours. And yes, it was as awful as it sounds.

But like most young professionals, I was doing what it took for me to get my start. In my case, that often meant early mornings and late nights at the office. Every day was a grind, and even at my age, it took everything out of me.

My father didn't need to be on that bus. He was in the later stretch of his career. He had greater control of his schedule and didn't have to be in the office that early. Most days, he didn't need to stay late either. Before I started taking the bus, he took his car into the city each day at times that avoided rush hour altogether.

But once I started going, he asked me, "Billy, what bus are you on?" And without making a big show of it, he was there, right next to me, sharing the ride into the city.

He didn't do it because it was convenient. He didn't do it because he had to. He did it because it created time together. And when the day was over—even if he could have left hours before—he waited to head home just so we could ride the same bus together again. Day by day, bus ride after bus ride, he was there. He didn't come with a life lesson or a long lecture. He just gave me his time—and it meant the world.

But he didn't just do this with me. Dad went above and beyond to spend time with my brother and sister as well. When he was in his late sixties, he put 1,300 miles on his new Harley just to participate in the annual biker rally in Sturgis, South Dakota, with my brother—all because motorcycles are one of my brother's great passions. It was quality time spent with my brother creating memories they'd never forget.

Dad also spent a lot of time with my sister and her family almost every day. Something I'll always remember is how he and my sister did the annual Christmas shopping for my mother's gifts. He certainly could have done this on his own, but doing it with my sister meant he got one-on-one time with her. And for my sister, it meant she ended up with almost as many presents as our mother. My father simply loved taking the time to give of himself, be present, and enjoy the people he cared about.

It sounds small, but this simple act spoke volumes. That time on the bus said more than any words ever could. It was an investment in me. It was love, spelled the way Zig Ziglar said children (and really all of us) spell it: T-I-M-E.

What I've come to realize from my father's example is that time, not money, is the most generous thing we can give—especially when we don't have to or when we could be somewhere else. We tend to talk about generosity in financial terms. Money is easy to quantify and easy to celebrate. Writing a check, sponsoring a cause, or putting your name on a donor wall—that kind of giving is visible. And for people with means, it's easy and doesn't actually cost them much. It's not a real sacrifice.

But giving your time? That's something else entirely. Time is the most valuable asset we have because it's the one thing we can't replenish. No matter who you are, you don't get to earn more of it. Once it's spent, it's gone. When you give someone your time, it makes a real statement. It's a quiet but undeniable signal that says, *I could be doing anything right now, yet I'm choosing to be here with you.* That kind of message carries more weight than any donation ever could. And it's why time is the true measure of generosity.

However, our culture seems to reflect the opposite. In the name of efficiency, we prioritize automation and delegation.

We treat relationships like transactions—things to check off, box up, or outsource. We hire professional movers instead of offering to help each other move. We put our elderly relatives into living facilities instead of choosing to spend time with them and care for them. We even joke about it, saying, "Just send someone" or "Just write the check."

But the truth is this: You can't delegate care. You can't outsource presence. You either show up, or you don't.

My dad didn't have to explain that to me. He showed it through consistent, quiet action. He didn't need to rearrange his schedule for me, but he did. He didn't need to give up that time, but he gave it anyway. He showed up, and by showing up, he showed me how to demonstrate value.

If you want to get an idea of what someone values most, don't look at their bank statements or credit card bills. Look at their calendars—how they spend their time—and you'll see what they value above all else.

It all starts with time. The question is this: *Are you spending your time in ways that actually matter?*

THE COST OF SHARING (AND NOT SHARING) YOUR TIME

We all can agree that time is our most valuable asset. That's why the moment we're asked to give it away, we hesitate. Giving your time comes with real tension, and in a world that constantly urges us to move faster, squeeze more in, and keep our calendars full, choosing to slow down and give time to others can feel inefficient or even wasteful.

One of our biggest hold-backs is fear. We don't like the idea of wasted investment. We only have so many hours in the day, and giving them away without a guarantee of return feels risky. We ask ourselves:

What if I mentor this team member and they leave the company?

What if I invest in this client relationship only for them to take their business elsewhere?

What if I give someone hours of my attention but they don't grow, don't care, or don't reciprocate?

Those are all fair questions. But here's another one: *What if you don't invest the time at all?* In my view, that's the real risk. Investing your time in other people regardless of the outcome is rarely a waste of time. You do what's right simply because it's right. You can't live in fear of something not working or someone leaving. In fact, people are more likely to stay if you do invest your time in them because you're offering them a brighter future.

When we withhold our time out of fear, we don't just miss a chance to help someone grow. We end up settling for underdevelopment and disengagement inside our own teams.

Fear is one barrier to time generosity. But another source of resistance is cultural. We live in a time of maximum efficiency. Entire industries are built on helping us do more with less, on making every process and interaction more efficient. We want there to be less effort, less contact, and less friction. We've trained ourselves to measure generosity by output, not presence. So when we're asked to give time instead of something easier and more efficient, we flinch at the thought.

But true generosity isn't just efficient. It's about building relationships and making connections. It's about spending time in person with someone. It's about a father choosing to ride the bus into the city with his son instead of taking his car.

In business especially, the pressure is real. There's always a deliverable to hit, a metric to track, or a system to perfect. Why spend the afternoon coaching a struggling coworker when you could just send him an explainer video? Why fly to see a client in person when Zoom is right there? Spending unnecessary time on someone runs counter to those goals, so we convince ourselves that we'll get around to it later when we have some extra time to spare. But *later* rarely comes. And in the meantime, we miss the very moments that matter most.

I remember a time when I got a call asking me to coach my daughter's junior high school soccer team. The position was supposed to go to a teacher, but no one wanted the job. I had coached those girls before, so I was the next call. *My first reaction?* "There's no way!" I was running a law firm. I couldn't be on the field every afternoon at 3:30 or riding a school bus to away games. It just didn't seem possible.

But when I thought about what it would mean to those girls if I did show up, I resolved to find a way. *And I did.* It was ten weeks of juggling practices and games, rearranging meetings, and pushing through exhaustion. But in the end, I knew it was worth it.

A few years later, I watched that team win the New Jersey state championship. I can't tell you how proud I felt. *Wow! Was that a great investment of my time!*

That experience showed me that the things that seem impossible often just require a decision. However, I also know how hard it is to be generous with your time. Time generosity requires something internal. It takes energy, intention, and an emotional investment. And when you already feel stretched thin, the idea of giving more than you already have feels impossible.

That's especially true when the return isn't immediate. If you mentor a colleague, you may not see signs of growth until months or even years later. You may never get credit for the impact, and in a world obsessed with recognition and results, that can make time generosity feel invisible.

So we guard our calendars. We ration our availability. We convince ourselves that keeping our distance is smarter, safer, and more sustainable. But here's the danger: The very act of protecting our time also isolates us from the people and moments that could be the most meaningful.

When we choose convenience over giving our time, we risk building shallow relationships. We're left with the kinds of relationships where people don't really know you, and you don't really know them.

It also means we miss out on moments of joy. We often forget that life happens in the margins—in the time that falls outside our systems of efficiency. It happens in the extra hour you spend mentoring a younger colleague or patiently discussing a situation with a client. It happens when you pause your busy schedule to lend a hand to a friend who appreciates it more than you'll ever know.

Those moments rarely show up on performance reviews, but they're the moments people remember. They're the ones you'll wish you'd made more time for when you look back on your life.

And here's the irony: We think that by guarding our time we'll be able to protect ourselves from exhaustion. But it's usually the opposite. When we only ever give our time to tasks, not people, we burn out faster. It's the human side of what we do—the connection, the care, the shared moments—that actually sustain us. Without that time, all we have is output. But output without meaning leads to fatigue and unfulfillment.

So, yes, giving your time may come with a cost. There's risk. There's tension. But the cost of not giving your time—the risk of superficial relationships, missed moments, and loss of purpose—is far worse.

LITTLE MOMENTS WITH BIG IMPACT

By the time I was in high school, my father had already worked himself through the hardest years of his life—juggling multiple jobs, going to school, and doing whatever it took to support our family. But even once things did become more stable, he didn't hoard his comfort. He gave it away in the form of time.

I've mentioned before how Dad often left our house with five unfinished projects of his own to go help out a neighbor who was building a deck, putting on an addition, or fixing something up. The neighbor might mention that he was working on a project one day. The next morning, my dad would grab his tool belt and show up at their house with no invitation. "Want some company?" he asked. "Let me give you a hand."

People felt that. They knew it was real because you can't fake that kind of presence. You either give it or you don't. And when you do, it sticks with people.

I remember the tailgates Dad hosted before the Jets games. He had incredible setups with a trailer full of food, drinks, chairs, and whatever else you might want. He spent hours prepping, hosting, feeding, and laughing with people in that parking lot. He missed the start of the game just to make sure everyone else was having a great time. After the game, he'd roll it all back out so no one had to sit in traffic.

He gave away his time like it was the most renewable resource in the world—but we all knew it wasn't. That might be why it meant so much.

When I gave the eulogy at my father's funeral, I kept coming back to how he always made time for people. He didn't just do it when it was easy; he made time even when it was inconvenient for him. It wasn't because he had something to gain. It was because he believed that's what people do for each other.

I've tried to follow that model in my own life—not just at home but in business too. When I take on a new client, especially if they're running a business, I don't just want to review their documents or sit on a conference call. I want to walk the factory floor. I want to meet their team, see their operation, and hear their story in their own space. That's how you make people feel seen and understood. That's how you build trust.

People are often surprised when I tell them that. They'll say, "You're really going to fly here just to see our operation?"

"Yes," I say, and I mean it. I often still sense some hesitation. *Uh-oh,* they think. *The lawyer wants to show up so he can bill me.* But I make it clear: "This is on my dime. I'm not billing you for a visit. I'm investing in our relationship."

I've flown across the country to see potential clients who weren't even sure they'd need my help. I just figured that if I was really going to put my best foot forward and be the kind of person I say I am, I had to do that in person. In nearly every one of those cases, not only did I earn the client, I earned the relationship—relationships I still have to this day.

I don't do it as part of a grand strategy; I do it because I want to be a person who's all about relationships. It's a way of moving through the world that says, *I want to understand you before I try to serve you.*

I do the same thing with people I mentor. Whether it's walking someone through a negotiation, showing them the "why" behind a strategy, or just sitting down and listening when they feel overwhelmed, I try to show up by freely giving them my time. *Why?* Because I remember what it felt like to have someone ride the bus with me when they didn't have to.

It's not always efficient. It's rarely convenient. But when you show others that you value them by giving them your time, it's worth it.

HOW TO MAKE YOUR TIME COUNT

Being generous with your time doesn't require making grand gestures. All you need to do is consistently show up in ways that are felt, not just seen. And that requires time.

But even when you start with the best intentions, giving your time is rarely convenient. The scarcity of time is what makes it meaningful, but it's also what makes it difficult.

Most people already feel stretched. When you look at your calendar, the day feels full before it ever begins. Giving your time can feel like an expense you can't afford, but what often looks like a costly detour is actually the best path forward.

Learning to be generous with your time takes a shift in mindset. The shift happens when you stop thinking about time as something you lose and start thinking about it as something you invest. When you approach your time as a gift you can give, it helps you allocate it with greater purpose.

Bob Burg and John David Mann describe this mentality as being a "Go-Giver." Most people approach relationships as "Go-Getters," asking, "What can I get?" But Go-Givers flip the question and ask, "What can I offer?"

The return on this kind of generosity doesn't always show up right away, if at all. The time you spend mentoring someone else might not change anything this month. That client visit might not result in a signed deal tomorrow. But in the long run, these moments build a worthy return on investment—a character-driven reputation.

A reputation for time generosity is powerful. People remember who showed up for them. They know they can go to you in good times and bad. They remember the times you stayed late to talk through a tough call and the times you flew out to see their business in person.

Time generosity sustains you too. When your calendar is filled with people rather than only deadlines, your energy changes. You feel more excited for the day ahead because you're grounded in meaning. Even the hard days carry weight and worth.

Whether it's my team, mentees, or the people who look to me for guidance, they warrant more than just a set of instructions; they deserve visibility, availability, and intentionality. Whether it's hallway chats, walks to lunch, or just time spent together, I make sure to be present for them.

I also audit my calendar and ask myself, *Does this reflect the people and things I value most?* If my schedule doesn't leave space for me to give time to others, it's going to be hard to live a life of meaningful connection. I know that sometimes I might need to say no to a few good things to make room for the right ones such as giving time to the people I love. As a business owner, it's too easy to give my best to my work and only leftovers to my family, but presence at home is the foundation of everything I do. Time with my family and friends isn't the excess I have once I've done everything else. It's a matter of first priority.

If I know my time will be tight during a certain season, I schedule generosity the way I schedule anything else that's important to me—in thirty-minute blocks here and there to ensure that I'm being generous with my time. I like to use that time to call someone who's been on my mind, to drop by a coworker's office just to check in, or to invite someone to lunch. I try not to overthink it or make it perfect. I just show up.

Finally, I consider the time I can invest with mentors. You're never too experienced to learn something from others. Being generous doesn't mean only looking downward. The people who challenge me, inspire me, and expand my thinking deserve my presence too. Time spent with someone who sharpens me is never wasted.

But none of this works if I'm overcommitted. Generosity requires having some margin. I've learned that when you say yes to everyone, you're actually saying no to the people who matter most. That's why one of the most generous things you can do is say no when you need to so you can say yes more fully.

Presence doesn't always feel productive. But it's almost always remembered. Maya Angelou famously said, "I've learned that people will forget what you said, people will forget what you did, but people will never forget how you made them feel." I say, people might forget what you said or did, but they will remember how it felt *when you made time for them*—when you paused your day, looked them in the eye, and stayed long enough to make it personal. That's what people hold onto. That's what sticks.

Dad at Sturgis Bike Week in South Dakota

Chapter 8

BE PRESENT

The Art of Asking Questions, Listening, and Following Up

One of the things I remember most clearly about my dad was his uncommon ability to be truly present. When he was with you, he was *completely* with you. No wandering attention. No glancing at a phone. No waiting for his turn to speak. When he offered you his time, it meant you had his full attention. And that presence made people feel like they mattered.

I remember one story that especially demonstrates this quality in Dad. It's a story my wife and I still laugh about to this day. She and I were spending some time with him, and the two of them were having a conversation, as they often did. Dad was being his usual engaged self. He was asking thoughtful questions, actively listening with genuine curiosity, and trying to follow up on her responses.

This time, however, she wasn't quite dialed in. Her attention had drifted, and it was clear to my father that she wasn't fully there. "Jen . . . Jen, I'm right here!" he said with a laugh.

It was a gentle nudge to pull her back into the moment, and he got a kick out of it. "Oh, sorry!" she responded, having realized she had been distracted.

Of course, my father wouldn't do this with just anybody, but with someone like Jen, he knew he could poke some fun.

It's easy to miss the significance of a moment like that. But looking back, I realize how rare and valuable that kind of presence is. My dad didn't need attention; he just valued people enough to let them know they had his.

When he talked to you, you could sense that you had all of him. And in return, you gave more of yourself. Conversations with my father often went deeper than you expected. That's what presence does. It opens the door.

It started with his incredible ability to ask the right questions—the kind that made you feel understood before you even answered.

Then he followed up. In the initial conversation, he asked insightful questions that made you feel further understood. But in the days and weeks to follow, your conversations with him would circle back to the original one—proving that he remembered what you said and that he was paying attention to you the first time. More than anything, it proved that you mattered to him.

Presence is built in moments like these. It's in the moments when you could easily drift but choose not to or when you decide to care about what someone else is saying and truly listen instead of simply waiting for your turn to speak. It happens when you pick up on a person's tone, when you ask a question that invites more, and when you bother to remember their answer.

My dad was especially good at reading between the lines. If someone was only half there in a conversation, he noticed it immediately. He didn't catch those things because he was judging people; he noticed because he wasn't distracted.

His presence wasn't loud. It wasn't about charisma or showmanship. He just paid attention on purpose. And when I think about the kind of leader, colleague, friend, and father I want to be, that model comes to mind. You don't need to be someone who dominates the room—just someone who makes others feel comfortable in it.

Most people don't think of presence as a professional skill. Instead, we tend to value things like credentials, strategy, vision, and results. But I would argue that one skill you need more than any of these is the ability to be truly present.

In a world where so few people are truly present, that ability becomes a superpower.

I've seen this to be the case in my own life and work. When you ask people good questions, listen with your full attention, and follow up with care, they notice. They respond differently. They open up. They trust you more.

And presence—*real* presence—is what's needed to make people feel like they are present.

THE COST OF INATTENTION

Several years ago, a colleague and I were meeting with a client who was dealing with a difficult employment law matter. The client was walking us through the details—what had happened, how it affected him, and the kind of resolution he was hoping for. These conversations are rarely easy. They require trust, emotional bandwidth, and a sense that the person across the table is really listening.

There was no question I was tuned in. I did what I always do when meeting clients: I left my phone on silent in my briefcase to eliminate any risk of distraction. Giving the client my full attention was important to both me and him. I wanted to ensure that I heard him and that he *felt* truly understood, and all of my body language communicated that.

But while I was tuned in, a quick glance over at my colleague told me he was not. I was mortified. He kept glancing at his phone even though it was clear that our client was emotionally distressed and needed to know he could trust us with this delicate matter. They were just quick glances, but enough for the client—and me—to notice.

That small gesture spoke volumes: *Something else is more important than you.* The trust in the room shifted.

We've all seen moments like this—and if we're honest, we've all had them. We live in a world that gives us every excuse not to be present. In our digital age, there's always something buzzing, pinging, or pulling at our attention. We juggle conversations while checking email inboxes. We listen while thinking about how to respond. We nod while our minds are five steps ahead or somewhere else entirely.

Over time, these habits start to shape our relationships.

It's not just about etiquette. It's about trust. When someone's telling you something that matters to them— whether it's a legal issue, a career decision, or something that happened with their kid—they're not just sharing information. They're offering a little piece of themselves. If that moment is met with distraction, they notice. And they pull back.

It doesn't take much. A sideways glance, a half-listened response, or the telltale shift of the eyes toward a screen is all it takes. These are small signals, but they add up quickly. And when they do, people stop opening up. They stop believing that you care. You may keep the conversation going on the surface, but the depth is gone.

The hardest part is that most of these lapses are unintentional. We're not trying to be dismissive. We're just tired, impatient, distracted, or rushed. But intent doesn't matter nearly as much as impact, and the impact of our inattention is disconnection.

The damage comes in a thousand almost-listening moments that chip away at trust. People pick up on your patterns. They can tell when you're not really there, and even if they never say it, the shift begins. Conversations get shorter. Feedback fades. Trust erodes.

So when they find someone who listens, it stands out.

It's tempting to think of presence as a luxury—something we'll give when we have more time or fewer distractions. But that couldn't be further from the truth. Presence is *essential*.

It's not what you offer after you've handled everything else. It's what makes everything else possible.

BUILT ON PRESENCE

Long before I ever sat across from a client or led a meeting, my dad taught me how to be present. He never sat me down and explained the mechanics of eye contact or active listening. He just lived it. While other fathers would have half-hearted conversations as they read the newspaper or watched the ball game on TV, my father was always fully present. And by watching him over time, I absorbed his ability to be in the moment with someone.

My father had an uncanny ability to draw people in. You could talk to him about anything, and you'd feel the full weight of his interest. You never wondered if he was thinking about something else. You never questioned whether he cared.

There was no doubt about it.

I watched him do it with friends, neighbors, coworkers, and clients. And I experienced it firsthand. When I went to him to try to figure something out, he wouldn't immediately offer a solution. He'd ask questions, and he'd help me find my way to clarity by talking it through. That kind of patience requires discipline. It takes someone who isn't trying to prove they're right but values understanding over control. That was my dad to a tee.

As I got older, I began to realize just how much presence builds trust. Psychology shows that a shift happens when someone is fully present with you. You're able to trust that person much more quickly. Something about their focus, care, and willingness to listen signals that they care about what matters to you.

And while society keeps moving faster and faster, that truth hasn't changed. We can have all the technology in the world, but at the end of the day, the relationships that matter will depend on your ability to be present.

That's why I've tried to carry my dad's model of presence into my own work and life. At my best, I'm asking thoughtful questions, listening without rushing to a solution, and circling back to check in. It sounds simple, but it's often more challenging than it seems, especially in a world where urgency and output outrun care.

But presence isn't about speed. It's about focus. When someone sits across from me, I try to remember what it feels like to be fully listened to, and I do my best to offer that same experience in return. It's not a tactic to win them over; it's just the kind of person I want to be.

That kind of listening takes work. It requires setting aside the part of your brain that's already solving the problem and generating responses, and instead focusing completely on the person in front of you. It's a muscle I'm still building. But when I do it well, everything changes. The tone shifts, the conversation deepens, and trust grows.

A few years ago, our firm tried to put into words what has made us successful—not just financially but in terms of our impact and longevity. What we landed on was simple: *Built on relationships, focused on results.*

It isn't just a tagline; it's the truth. Everything we've built has come from the trust we've earned over time—a trust that never could have happened if we weren't committed to asking questions, listening well, and following up.

THE KEY TO SHOWING UP

As I've said, the true measure of generosity is the way you give of your time for other people. And true generosity happens when you set everything else aside—every distraction, every notification, every thought competing for your attention— and choose to be fully there for someone else. In my mind, that's what presence is—giving your time *and* attention. It's not a ploy or a tactic. It's just a quiet way of saying, *You matter more than whatever else I could be doing right now.*

More than that, when my goal is to communicate to someone that I'm really available to them, I work to ask better questions. I actually listen to the answers. And then I follow up in a way that shows I was paying attention the first time.

I've found that a good question—one that's not designed to impress but to uncover something real—you give the other person a path to go deeper. There's one question I've come back to again and again in all kinds of settings: "What's your ideal outcome?"

Asking this kind of question creates room. It doesn't lead the witness. It doesn't assume you already know what they're after. It just invites them to start laying it out. People tend to say something unexpected when you give them space like that—something they hadn't even fully said out loud until that moment. I find myself understanding not just their situation but their priorities and the things that are really driving their thinking. That's what curiosity does; it opens doors that you didn't even know were there.

Genuine curiosity demonstrates that you already have an interest in and care for the person in front of you, even if you may not know them yet. And having that kind of interest and care comes from something deeper, something more fundamental. It's a belief that everyone matters— your kids, your partner, your friends, your colleagues, your clients, everyone.

When my wife and I were designing our home, I received a question like this from our architect. Before we ever got into square footage or cost, he told us, "Tell me everything you'd want in a perfect world. Don't worry about the constraints yet. Just describe your ideal."

So we did—an open staircase, a butler's pantry, a home gym, a wine cellar. We rattled off a whole list of things we didn't think we could actually have. We didn't assume he'd be able to make all those things work, but to our surprise, he came back with a design that included it all.

That approach stuck with me because it's exactly how I try to serve my clients. If I assume I know what they want, I'll likely miss it. But if I ask them to define success in their own words, I can shape everything I do around getting them there.

It's a simple question, but most people never ask it. They're too quick to solve and too quick to advise. But building trust requires slowing down and starting with that kind of question.

After I ask a good question, I stop talking and just listen. As my dad used to say, "We have two ears and one mouth so we can listen twice as much as we speak." I think he stole that from Mark Twain—or maybe Twain stole it from someone else. Either way, it stuck with me because it's really true.

The hardest part of listening isn't hearing the words. It's resisting the urge to jump in, especially if you're an ideas person and just want to help. In my profession, that urge is everywhere. And to be honest, a lot of lawyers love the sound of their own voice. They want to be the smartest person in the room. They interrupt. They finish your sentences. They start responding before you've even finished talking. And they often don't even realize they're doing it.

But when you jump in too soon because you're not really present, you miss the point. You're not listening to understand; you're listening for a pause so you can speak. I've had to train myself not to jump ahead, not to start forming a solution in my head before the person even tells me what they really want. It's a discipline, and it takes practice. But the people who get it right are the ones others want to keep talking to.

Of course, none of it means much if you don't follow up. After all the good questions and attentive listening—being present—I always circle back. It might be a few days later, a week, or even a month. But checking in and making it clear that I remembered what someone told me sends this message: *What you shared stuck with me.*

Again, it doesn't have to be a grand gesture. In fact, the smaller it is, the more sincere it might feel. But the point is that I just reach out. Sometimes it's a quick note, a text, or a simple "Hey, how did that thing go?"

I've found that when I bring up topics in conversation that a client told me about weeks prior, they light up. *Wow!* they think. *He remembered.* That simple gesture shows them that they matter enough for you to carry that thread forward.

That's the kind of presence people don't forget.

And here's the thing: It won't be perfect. You'll miss things. You'll get distracted. But presence is a muscle. The more you use it, the stronger it gets. Eventually, it becomes not something you *do*—it's who you *are*.

My friend, mentor, and partner, Barry Mandelbaum

Chapter 9

PLAY THE LONG GAME

The Path to Dealing with Difficult People

When I first joined the firm that would eventually become Mandelbaum Barrett—back when it was still a twenty-lawyer outfit—I was young, ambitious, and ready to build something. I had just come from one of the world's biggest firms, but I was looking for a space where I could use my entrepreneurial instincts. I didn't have a book of business yet. All I had was my work ethic, my love of building personal relationships, and a drive to make something happen.

Most people at the firm welcomed me. But one partner decided early on that he didn't want me there. It wasn't because

I had done anything wrong, and it wasn't like we had any real conflict. In fact, he didn't even know me. From what I could tell, he just didn't like how quickly I was gaining traction.

I didn't hear it from him directly. I first heard it from a partner I'd grown close to—someone who took on a mentor role in those early days. He pulled me aside one day and told me what was being said behind closed doors.

The partner had been going around saying I wasn't impressive, that my credentials didn't matter, that I wasn't as smart as people thought I was, and that I was just a salesman.

To be clear, I was only twenty-seven years old. I was still learning the business of law. I hadn't brought in big clients yet, but I was hustling—calling everyone I knew, trying to get introductions, and looking for opportunities to prove myself. I wasn't trying to step on toes. I was just working hard and learning my craft.

So when I heard what this partner was saying, I was frustrated, not just because it was unfair but because I couldn't understand the motive. There was no reason for it. It seemed like it was just quiet, petty sabotage.

But what could I do? Would I call him out? Should I pull others in to defend me? Do I leave the firm altogether?

I didn't do any of those things.

I did what my father taught me to do—kill him with kindness—not because he deserved it or because it felt good. I did it because it was the right thing to do. It kept me grounded. It kept me focused. And in the long run, *it always worked.* So I smiled, said hello, treated him respectfully, and went about my business. If anything, my motivation for success was only further amped up. Just like when I had something to prove after I didn't get into a top ten law school in the first round of applications, the big chip on my shoulder was definitely back.

I focused on what I *could* control. I put my head down and worked. I stayed responsive. I built relationships. I looked for opportunities, and when they came, I followed through.

Slowly, I started learning my craft as a business lawyer and bringing in clients. They weren't massive at first, but they steadily grew. I was proving I could create relationships and instilling confidence that my clients could rely on me as their lawyer and trusted advisor. And little by little, people began to notice—not just the work, but the way I handled myself. They noticed that I didn't complain, gossip, or play games. I just kept showing up, doing the work, and trying to grow.

Most people are intuitive and eventually figure out what you are all about. So as that partner continued with his toxic, negative attitude, the new lawyers in the firm came to see him for what he was and were turned off by it. Over time, the contrast became increasingly obvious.

The more I focused on becoming a better lawyer—consistently maintaining a positive attitude and engaging in a culture of building up the people around me—the more credibility I gained. Meanwhile, the partner never changed, but the perception around him did. And that shift had nothing to do with confrontation. It had everything to do with time and consistency. Eventually, that other partner became less and less relevant until he retired. That experience was early practice for how I handle difficult people to this day.

The reality is that there are people in every ecosystem who don't want to see you succeed. They might be insecure. They may be competitive. They may be jealous. Or maybe they just don't like change. Whatever their reason, they'll work—either subtly or overtly—to hold you back.

It's tempting to fight them, to expose what they're doing, or to go toe-to-toe and set the record straight. But most of the time, that's a trap. The second you get drawn into the mess, you've lost. You've let someone else dictate your behavior. And whether you win the argument or not, you've lost time, energy, and focus that could've gone into actually building something.

I believe that dealing with difficult people well is one of the clearest signs of maturity. Anyone can treat someone well when they're being treated well in return. But how you act when someone's trying to undercut you is the test.

You can lash out, you can retreat, or you can hold your ground and keep doing excellent work. That's the long game.

I didn't beat that toxic partner by arguing with him or matching his tactics. I *outlasted* him. And I did it by being someone others could trust, respect, and count on.

If you're facing someone like that—someone who's making things harder than they need to—don't panic. Don't get petty. And don't lower your standards just because someone else already has.

Instead, play the long game. Eventually, the difference between you and them will speak for itself.

WHEN RESPECT ISN'T EASY

The greatest challenges in your career often come from sources other than the work itself. They come in the form of people who are incredibly difficult to navigate.

You know the type. You've probably worked with them throughout your life already. They're the combative ones, the demanding ones, the ones who seem to go out of their way to make things difficult. They're the people who feel like human sandpaper, and every interaction with them grates on you.

Throughout my career, I've had clients who were impossible to please and colleagues who felt like they needed to compete with everyone. You can try to avoid those people as much as you can, but it's not always possible.

In fact, the more responsibility you take on, the more of those people you're bound to encounter. Some have power. Some have proximity. And whether you like it or not, some have influence over your success.

When someone is unpleasant but irrelevant, it's easy to walk away. But when you're stuck in meetings with them, when they hold authority over you, or when they are a client or customer, you can't just opt out. You still have to show up, deliver, and find some way to work with them.

If you don't have a plan for how to deal with people like that, the toll can be real. I've seen good people who have slowly fallen apart under the weight of impossible relationships. At first, it's just frustration or resentment, but eventually it becomes exhaustion. And when people get exhausted, they lose focus and clarity. They stop thinking about the big picture and start fixating on the next frustrating encounter. All this tension builds—even when they're not around the person who caused it. And it changes how they show up until they inevitably blow up or burn out.

I've watched professionals lose their cool in meetings and undo years of credibility in one moment. And I've seen talented people give up entirely, letting their work suffer because they were so sick of the tension.

When someone's pushing your buttons—whether they're passive-aggressive or just outright rude—it takes everything in you not to respond in kind.

When that happens, they're not the only difficult one. *Now you're part of the conflict too.*

That's how reputation damage begins. When you let difficult people set the tone, you open the door to slow erosion of professionalism that progresses over time.

I'm not saying you should tolerate abuse. If someone crosses a line, you need to protect yourself. Don't go so far as to compromise your integrity or allow someone to run over you in the name of being professional.

But most of the time, that's not the case. It's tension in the room and conversations that never go the way they should. And the real question becomes, *How do you carry yourself in that environment?*

Your response will define your trajectory.

WINNING PEOPLE OVER

A lot of how I learned to deal with people goes back to how I was raised. My dad's philosophy was that those in authority—whether teachers, coaches, or bosses—deserved respect, even when they weren't easy to deal with.

He used to tell me, "They're right, even when they're wrong." As a kid, that was hard to understand. But he wasn't saying those authority figures were perfect. It was just that he believed learning how to operate within someone else's authority was part of growing up. And it was good training for life.

He didn't want me to ignore conflict or unfair treatment. But he wasn't going to fix it for me either. It was a lesson in learning how to manage tension with maturity. He believed that figuring out how to handle people by working through personality clashes and navigating relationships with grace were some of the most important skills a person could develop.

He was right. And as I got older, I saw exactly what he was talking about. It started with school and sports, but it didn't stop there. Those same patterns showed up in the workplace and the business world.

If you haven't already, at some point in your career you'll have to deal with bosses, clients, or colleagues who are difficult. There's no avoiding it. And when that time comes, you'll have to figure out how to keep showing up and doing your job anyway.

That was my dad's experience too. He had a boss, Al Vaccaro, who most people had trouble with. The guy was tough, demanding, and short-tempered. But my dad didn't avoid him. Instead, he learned how to work with him. He figured out what made Al tick and focused on what he could learn.

My father figured out that what Al liked more than anything was looking good to upper management, so he took every opportunity to do things that made Al look good. He covered for Al, did whatever he was asked to do, and did it extremely well with a smile. He spoke well of Al in front of those who were listening, and he went so far as to be a cheerleader for him to upper management, always showing respect for him and his position—even though nobody else did.

Ultimately, my father became a hero to Al, who not only taught him a lot over the years but also supported my dad's advancement in the company—something he had not done often for others. Even though their relationship wasn't warm, my dad learned how to make it productive. He became a hero to the guy nobody liked or could work with. And that was enough. Eventually he surpassed Al within the company.

My father never made excuses for difficult people, but he never wasted energy resenting them either. He stayed calm. He stayed focused. And he kept doing the job. That steady, composed, and respectful posture is one I've tried to carry forward in my own life as well.

When you learn how to handle people well, you don't just survive those relationships; you grow through them. You build trust, a reputation, and the kind of respect that lasts. If you can win over the most difficult people, you can build a relationship with anyone.

A RESPONSE THAT RESOLVES THINGS

Difficult people don't have to derail you or your success. But they do require something from you—patience, discernment, and the willingness to handle tension without letting it handle you.

You can't always avoid these people. You can't always out-charm them. And you can't necessarily count on them changing. What you can control is how you carry yourself—the way you respond regardless of the way others do.

It's not something you can master overnight. It's a skill that you grow into. But from my experience over the years, I've discovered that a few steady practices have made all the difference in how I work with people who make life harder than it needs to be.

First, stay kind even when it's not reciprocated. When someone's rude, short, or dismissive, your instincts will want to kick in. You'll either want to fight back or pull away. But both reactions give them control. What actually disarms people while also protecting your credibility is showing up calmly and professionally, no matter how they act.

I've had people challenge me in meetings, belittle my work, and even do things to try to provoke a response. What they never expect is continued composure. I stay steady. I don't raise my voice, and I don't get passive-aggressive. Instead, I engage in respectful dialogue.

The interesting thing is that when you do that, it tends to shift the room. People notice who works with kindness and professionalism and who doesn't.

For example, our firm once worked on a major transaction for one of our client companies that was being purchased by a large private equity group. It was a complicated transaction with a lot of money at stake, and the large, national law firm representing the other side made it their business to be incredibly difficult. They constantly raised issues and problems, seemingly creating issues where none existed. It was the typical behavior that makes most people dislike attorneys.

But instead of fighting fire with fire, we kept our cool throughout the entire matter. We not only took the high road and maintained our demeanor and professionalism but we consistently kept suggesting solutions and fixes to the problems they raised. In essence, they were the problem-raisers, and we became the solvers who were always looking for win-win outcomes to their issues.

About two weeks after the deal closed, we got a call from the executives of the private equity group on the other side of the deal. They asked us to meet them for coffee. At the meeting, they told us that they recognized how difficult and combative their attorneys were and how they constantly created problems by raising issues that were not all that important to them. They noted how their attorneys found plenty of problems but offered no solutions. They were impressed that we consistently acted like deal-making professionals, offering fair solutions to every problem raised. As a result, they hired us to represent them in the future, and they continue to be one of our largest clients to this day.

You can't control how people treat you, but you can decide how you respond. And when you stay kind under pressure, you gain more than the upper hand. You gain respect in the eyes of others.

Second, pay attention to what matters most to them. Not every difficult person is out to cause problems. Some are just deeply tied to specific needs. If you can figure out what those are and address them head on, you take a lot of the heat out of the relationship.

Our firm once had a client—a very successful dentist who owned a dozen practices—who was widely known for being demanding. She expected immediate access to our team. She texted us at 3:00 a.m., including holidays, and wanted fast responses without exception. Most professionals couldn't handle her and gave up. There was a long list of previous advisors for whom it just didn't work out. But one of my partners, Casey, took a different approach.

Rather than get defensive or avoidant, Casey tried to understand what drove her behavior. What she saw was pretty straightforward: This client's core need was *responsiveness and immediate access*. She wanted to know that when something mattered, someone would be there.

So Casey made that her priority. She remained intentional. When the client sent her a message, she acknowledged the client quickly, even if the full answer came later. She deployed a level of hypervigilance in her speedy responses. In doing so, Casey built an unprecedented level of trust. She did something nobody else was able to do because she figured out that it wasn't the deliverable that had to occur instantly—just an acknowledgment that the client's note had been seen. The client was actually a bit more reasonable when that happened. For her, it was all about the immediate access to discuss whatever was pressing on her mind.

The result? A relationship that's lasted over five years and counting. It wasn't because the client changed but because Casey learned how to respond clearly and intentionally.

Third, deliver the way they need it. Working effectively with difficult people doesn't mean changing your standards, but it might mean adjusting your style.

Some people want every detail. Others just want to know you've got it handled. The key isn't to guess; it's to observe. Pay attention to how these difficult people in your life absorb information, what puts them at ease, and how they prefer to engage. You need to understand their ideal outcome first if you are to have any hope of delivering it.

Let's say you're trying to give feedback to a colleague. One person might respond well to directness. Just give it to them straight, and they'll appreciate your honesty. But someone else might shut down if you're too blunt. They need to hear what's working before they can absorb what needs to change. If you deliver the same message the same way to both people, you'll either bruise one or confuse the other.

If your goal is impact, not just expression, then how you say it matters as much as what you say. One size doesn't fit all. Deliver the way they need it.

You don't have to compromise your process or dumb down anything to do so. It is just about delivering value in a way they can actually receive it.

When you meet people where they are—especially the hard ones—you increase the odds of a productive relationship.

Fourth, don't just write it out; talk it through. I've seen time and again how emailing about conflicts makes problems worse, not better. Tension builds, tone gets misread, and what should have been a quick fix turns into a standoff. Meanwhile, no one's bothering to pick up the phone or, better yet, have a meeting.

Years ago, I was working on a transaction for my client to purchase a business. I was going back and forth with the seller's attorney, and it was going nowhere. Each email made things more complicated, and what should have been a relatively straightforward deal got increasingly drawn out—all in the name of a more "efficient" form of communication. With each email, it seemed like more issues kept popping up. He would start his messages with, "That is a deal-breaker for my client" or "That is a nonstarter." And each time, progress on the deal came to a screeching halt.

So I asked for an "all-hands call" and got both clients on the phone. I suggested that the four of us—both clients and attorneys—meet in a room in person with the current draft of the contract and go through it page by page to try to iron things out together. After all, both parties really wanted to make a deal.

The other side's client chimed in before his attorney could respond and said, "That's a great idea. Let's all meet and go through the agreement." The next week, we all met. We talked it through—just two professionals and their clients trying to get to the bottom of a deal. As we turned the pages and I politely framed each issue, it became clear that the other side's client couldn't care less about 90 percent of the issues, and one by one they dropped them as non-issues.

Thirty minutes later (literally that was it, only half an hour) after weeks of wasteful back and forth, the deal was done. Our positions weren't actually that far apart. We just couldn't see it through the screen. We literally had the changes made to the agreement, printed the pages, and executed the contract at that table the same day.

On its face, it doesn't seem like having an in-person meeting is such a magical suggestion, but letting the other side's client hear my demeanor and approach as a deal-maker and problem-solver who was just trying to help made all the difference.

So if you want to get to the bottom of things fast, don't just write it out. Talk it through.

Fifth, know where your lines are, and hold them. Another lesson I've learned over the years is that you don't have to take on every client who comes your way. In fact, you shouldn't.

There are relationships that wear you down more than they're worth. Some relationships will inevitably distract you, drain your time, and leave you second-guessing yourself. You might be able to manage them, but the cost adds up.

Earlier in my career, I said yes to just about everything. If a client was difficult, I saw it as a challenge. I'd figure out what made them tick and try to win them over. And a lot of times, I did. That approach helped me grow, and it sharpened my instincts.

But at this point in my career, I think differently. I can afford not to take on certain difficult people. It's not about whether I *can* make it work; it's whether it makes sense to.

This is especially important when it comes to matters of integrity. Know what you will and won't do, and stick to it. There have been times in the past when I've had to withdraw as the attorney in a deal and tell my client I would not be participating. "If that's the road you want to go down, you're welcome to go down it with someone else," I said. I then sent back my retainer fee and the client's file and wished him well.

You cannot compromise your professional ethics no matter how badly you want to help someone. And trust me, you won't lose anything by walking away from the wrong kind of relationship.

At the end of the day, if you can learn how to respond well to difficult people—by killing them with kindness, paying attention to what matters to them, delivering it in the way they need it, talking it through, and holding your boundaries—you'll become the kind of person people know they can count on. You'll create and keep relationships others can't, and you'll build a reputation that lasts.

Teenage years, playing baseball in the senior majors for Coach Dunny

Chapter 10

LEAVE A MARK FOR OTHERS

Your Fingerprints on Success

The greatest impact we have isn't what we achieve; it's who we influence. That's our real legacy. The fingerprints we leave on other people's success can last longer than anything we build ourselves.

One of the first people who left a fingerprint of success on me was my Little League baseball coach. His name was Jim Dunlop, but everyone called him Dunny.

I have one particular memory with Dunny that I'll never forget. I was about fourteen years old, and it was a senior majors playoff game, the bottom of the last inning. We had two outs with the bases loaded, and we were down by one run. I stepped into the batter's box with the season on the line.

By that point, I knew the routine. Before every pitch, you look to Dunny standing near third base for the sign. That's what he'd drilled into us. But when I looked over that time, he didn't move. He just stood there with a grin and said, "What the hell are you looking at me for? You gotta get a hit."

That was it. He knew he didn't need to give me a signal or a strategy. It was pretty obvious what I needed to do, but he had me trained to look for that sign every pitch. He believed I was ready. With that grin and lighthearted comment at the biggest moment in our season, he let me know it—just like that, plain and simple.

He was right. A moment later, I got the hit, and we won the game.

But the reason I remember that moment isn't because of the win (well, maybe it is just a little bit). It's because everything about it reflected who Dunny was and how he led and taught as a coach. He believed in preparing players with the fundamentals, in encouraging best efforts in execution, in taking responsibility for your particular job or role, and in turning average kids into something much more.

Dunny was a Vietnam War veteran and a mailman in our small town. While he had no kids of his own, he devoted himself to coaching youth sports and serving his community. In our town's Little League program, he built a dynasty. His teams won four straight championships in the Senior Majors division—a nearly impossible feat when a significant portion of your roster turns over every year as kids age out. I believe it is a record that still stands today some forty years later.

But his secret wasn't just finding talent. It was discipline. Dunny drafted B-level players and turned them into A-level performers. We practiced every day, even when other teams took the day off. When others waited for warm weather, we started in the cold days of early March. I can remember starting our spring practices with patches of snow still on the ground. We were always the first to start playing, and we practiced every day—no excuses. And if you didn't have a ride, Dunny would pick you up on his way to the field.

Dunny drilled the fundamentals relentlessly. If you made a mistake in a game, you practiced that play until it became second nature. He expected everyone to give their best effort, not excuses. If you hit a ground ball, you sprinted to first base as if the game depended on it. If you struck out and started pouting, he would call it out. "Come on, don't be a baby," he'd say. In other words, he held you to a higher standard because he believed you could meet it, and he knew what it took to be consistently successful.

Dunny was tough on us, but that never bothered my parents. To the contrary, they appreciated him because they knew he was keeping us accountable to make us better.

At the time, I didn't think about any of that. I was just a kid trying to play hard and not mess up. But years later, I realized Dunny wasn't just teaching us about baseball. He was preparing us for life, making us ready to show up when the moment mattered.

When the moment arrived for me to step up to the plate, I *was* ready. Dunny had done his job. He had prepared me. And when the time came, he stepped back and let me rise to the occasion.

I've thought about that story often over the years. And as I reflect, I realize that Dunny's fingerprints are all over the way I think, lead, and perform. His influence shows up when I'm tempted to play it safe, hold back, or overthink. Throughout life, you always want to be at bat with a chance to win the game. Those are the moments you live for.

That's the power of an intentional mentor—an impact that lasts longer than they ever realize. It's remarkable to think that such an impact could come from a Little League coach. It underscores just how impactful the impressions we make on people can be, even when we may not realize it.

Most of us are shaped by a handful of people who took the time to invest in us. Sometimes they do it through words. Sometimes it's action. Sometimes it's simply the example they set. You don't always notice it at the moment. But eventually you look back and realize how much of your life was influenced by someone else's presence.

And now, whether you realize it or not, you're doing the same thing for someone else. It's not just about recognizing who shaped you. It's also understanding that you're shaping others too.

Every conversation, every correction, every word of belief you offer has the potential to echo for years to come.

Right now, someone is watching how you carry yourself. Someone is learning how to handle pressure by watching how you respond to it. Someone is starting to believe they can—or can't—because of whether you believed in them first.

Your fingerprints are already on someone's life. The only question is what kind of mark you're leaving.

THE WRONG KIND OF FINGERPRINTS

Dunny showed up for us every single day. He continued to teach, correct, and encourage us more and more until the lessons finally took hold. But not everyone has a coach like that. And sometimes, even for those of us who had one, we can quickly forget what it means to be that kind of influence for someone else.

That's something I learned the hard way with my own son, Billy. He told us that he wanted to be a Division I football player. That was his dream. He had set his sights on it, and he was willing to do the work.

But what did I do? *I tried to steer him somewhere safer.*

I reminded him that he was also a great lacrosse player and that our town was known for its lacrosse program and not as much for football. I pointed out that many more people play football across all fifty states, so the chances of getting recruited for D1 football weren't nearly as good as they were for lacrosse. And I explained to him that kids from powerhouse high school programs in places like Texas and Florida or the large private and parochial schools that recruit players from other places had better odds since their schools got a lot more recruiting attention from the D1 programs.

In other words, I offered every reason why getting recruited for football would be harder to achieve than lacrosse—if not impossible. And while I truly believed in my heart that it was possible, perhaps I didn't think it was nearly as probable.

In my defense, I did it all with good intentions. I wasn't *trying* to discourage him. In my mind, I guess I was trying to stack the deck in his favor, protecting him from the possibility of disappointment and heartbreak. But in doing so, I became exactly the kind of voice I've spent my whole life trying to push back against. I did exactly what my father would not have done: I contradicted a value system and mindset that I'd spent a lifetime living.

I became my son's limiting voice.

As I think back, it actually blows my mind and makes me so disappointed in myself. I deeply and truly believe that nothing is beyond our reach, yet here I was doing exactly the thing I despise.

If that had come from a stranger or a peer, it would have been one thing. But when it comes from a parent—especially a parent who talks so much about possibility and resilience— that kind of doubt imposes more weight than it should.

Thankfully, Billy didn't listen. In spite of me, he kept working toward his dream. He kept believing. He stayed focused on his goal, even while I was nudging him toward a more "reasonable" path. And eventually, he produced the momentum. The right coach saw his film, gave him a recruiting visit, and believed he could compete at a high level. As a result, the right door opened at the right moment, and Billy got a Division I offer to play football.

He accepted it, and one of the first things he did was walk into his lacrosse coach's office and respectfully resign from the team midseason. "This isn't my path," he said. "I know that football is where I'm headed, and I want to completely dedicate and focus on that from now on."

Watching this story unfold up close and personal stopped me in my tracks. I had watched Billy do exactly what I had done in my own life—block out the noise, push through the doubt, believe anything can happen, and take the road other people said was too hard or maybe even impossible. It was an incredibly proud moment for me as a dad. And I realized how close I might have come to silencing that instinct in him. It was a humbling moment for me, and it's one that will stick with me forever.

Even those of us who make it our mission to be a hero to others aren't immune to slipping. We can all fall back into comfort, fear, and logic—especially when we care deeply about the person in front of us. But caring for someone doesn't mean shielding them. It means preparing them for what's ahead and demonstrating that you have faith in their ability to succeed.

My father understood that. He wasn't reckless or indifferent, but he never softened the world for me. He didn't put bumpers on every sharp edge. He believed in letting me struggle because he knew I would figure it out for myself. And knowing that he believed in me carried me farther than any protection ever could.

That's a hard lesson for anyone in a position of influence—parents, coaches, and business leaders alike. Every day, whether we realize it or not, we're influencing people. We're either expanding someone's view of what's possible or we're shrinking it. We're either giving people courage or we're feeding their caution. And if we're not intentional about that influence, we may leave fingerprints that we never meant to leave.

Sometimes those negative lessons show up in a missed opportunity or a goal that gets quietly abandoned. Sometimes they show up years later in the form of a story someone tells about the person who didn't believe in them. But other times—if we're lucky—we catch ourselves in time to change the story.

The truth is that there's often a gap between what we say we believe and how we actually lead. It's in that gap where people either rise or retreat. And if we want to lead well—in business, at home, or anywhere else—we have to be willing to face that gap. We have to be honest about when fear gets the best of us. And we have to commit to being the kind of voice that helps others move forward rather than pull back.

MENTORS WHO LEAVE A MARK

The most meaningful influences don't just inspire you. They reshape what you believe about yourself.

Growing up, I was lucky to have mentors who didn't simply offer advice. They offered belief. That belief changed the way I saw myself, the way I led, and the way I now try to show up for others.

My dad was one of those people. He didn't give me many pep talks or grand speeches. Instead, he modeled work ethic, steadiness, and quiet resilience in everything he did. You didn't hear him *talk* about grit—he just lived it.

He used to say, "There are two kinds of people in the world: winners and losers. Winners are the ones who find a way." That might sound harsh out of context, but I understood what he meant. He wasn't talking about beating other people. His point was that if you want to win, you have to refuse to be beaten by your circumstances.

That message shaped me. It taught me to press forward, even when the odds didn't look good. Throughout my career, there have been plenty of moments when people told me what I could and couldn't do.

They said I could not get accepted to Boston College, but I did *and* I made the dean's list. They said I wouldn't get into a top ten law school, but I did. They said I'd never get a job in a worldwide New York law firm, but I made it happen. And when I joined the Mandelbaum firm and started climbing the ladder, doubters even told me I'd never become a managing partner because my religion wasn't Judaism.

All those statements were supposed to be ceilings, but I didn't accept any of them.

In each of those moments, I carried those negative words with me—not as weights but as fuel. I made it my mission to prove them wrong. I believed there was more in me. And when that belief wavered, I leaned on the people who believed in me until I could believe in myself again.

Gary Young was one of those people. Gary was a partner at the firm that is now Mandelbaum Barrett back when I first joined. He's also the one who taught me the value of knowing a lot about a lot of things.

From the beginning, Gary served as a mentor to me. He took me everywhere with him. He showed me how to handle meetings and develop client relationships, and he gave me the opportunity to be the lead attorney on matters we handled together, even when I was a young associate lawyer. Gary patiently showed me the ropes while I was still getting the hang of things. He had confidence in me, and he let me know it. Gary made a point to tell anyone who would listen that I was a rising star. That kind of loyalty did more than provide opportunity; It built my confidence and told me that I was somebody worth developing. Gary helped me visualize a bigger, brighter future for myself, and he bolstered my confidence that I would eventually build a significant practice on my own.

Mr. Mandelbaum did something similar. Not long after I joined the firm, Mr. Mandelbaum gave me the opportunity to be the lead attorney on a major real estate deal even though many people disagreed with the decision. The project was the acquisition and development of a former horse racing track. My client was to buy the track, redevelop the site, and ultimately negotiate long-term leases with some big box stores. By all accounts, it was an involved and sophisticated real estate matter—not the kind that would usually go to someone so new and relatively inexperienced.

Until that moment, I was primarily handling business and corporate transactions. However, I had instilled a lot of confidence in the client, and they wanted me to handle the matter personally. Thankfully, Mr. Mandelbaum, the managing partner of the firm and the head of the real estate department, saw past my lack of experience and focused instead on my potential. He believed that if you had the brains and enough intellectual curiosity, you could do anything you put your mind to as an attorney. So he gave me a chance. And that chance changed everything. It didn't just make me a better lawyer; it helped me (and the naysayers) believe I belonged in the room and that although I was young, I could operate at the same level as partners in the firm.

Finally, I think about my good friend Dave Roth, a CPA who has been one of my best referral sources and a dear friend for nearly twenty-five years. In the early years of my career, Dave referred clients to me, and I always brought a senior attorney with me to instill confidence in the potential client or show that I had experienced people backing me up. Often, those early clients were closer to my parents' age, so I felt I needed to rely on older partners to bolster my opportunity.

After a couple years of sending me referrals, Dave sent me a new client opportunity, but this time he made a point to call me before the meeting. "Make it just you this time," he said. "You don't need to bring Gary or anyone else. You're as good or better than anyone you would bring. You're ready for this."

That was a moment I will never forget. Dave showed me he had confidence in me, which helped me believe it for myself. That was the last time I leaned on an older attorney to land a new relationship.

Those men didn't explicitly tell me how to dismantle limiting beliefs, but they did show me how to live without them. They didn't try to protect me from failure. They pushed me toward growth. They created space for me to rise.

And in return, I've done my best to be that for others. In my role as a business lawyer to entrepreneurs, that often means guiding people to realize their best potential and continue their journey toward bigger and better successes.

That's how you leave fingerprints that last. It's not through dramatic moments or big declarations. It's the small, consistent signals that make all the difference—whether it's someone choosing to trust you, challenge you, or see something in you before you can see it for yourself.

The people who shaped us didn't just leave lessons; they left their fingerprints on our success. They trusted us enough to occasionally drop us in the deep end and let us swim on our own, and that made all the difference.

Now, it's our responsibility to do the same. It's our job to be the kind of leaders whose fingerprints reflect belief and not fear, pushing people toward their potential instead of pulling them back toward what feels safe.

HOW YOU CRAFT YOUR LEGACY

When you look back on your life, the impact that matters most won't be the deals you closed, the championships you won, or the titles you earned. It will be the people you helped form—the ones who were better off because you showed up, believed in them, and gave them a chance even though you didn't have to. That's the real legacy. It's not about *what* you build but *who* you build.

None of us gets here alone. We've all had moments when someone chose to believe in us—whether we were ready or not. Maybe it was a boss who gave you a chance, a teacher who expected more from you, a coach who put the ball in your hand when the game was on the line, or a parent who challenged your excuses. Whatever it was for you, those moments became the anchors of confidence you needed to succeed on your own.

Now, as you craft your own legacy, you have the opportunity to do that for others. If that sounds like too heavy a responsibility, don't sweat it. People don't need perfection from you. All they need is someone who is willing to step in, pay attention, and say, "I see something in you, and I am not afraid to say so." That kind of belief, offered at the right time, has a way of leaving a profound mark.

It also has a way of compounding. The people who influenced me helped shape how I influence others. Their fingerprints show up in the way I lead, the way I speak to my kids, and the way I think about mentoring the next generation. Their investment didn't end with me, and yours won't either.

On the opposite side of the coin, when you withhold belief, even unintentionally, you shrink what others believe is possible. That can happen subtly by playing it safe, managing instead of mentoring, or letting fear drive decisions. Over time, that caution starts to undermine their self-confidence. You may tell yourself you are being responsible, but what you're really doing is lowering the ceiling for the people around you.

I've caught myself doing it on more than one occasion, and my son's story with Division I football is just one example. We all do it. We start defaulting to what is efficient instead of focusing on what is meaningful. But when you look back, you realize that the most meaningful things were rarely the efficient things you were focusing on.

Leaving the right kind of mark on others requires time, trust, and belief. And belief, like anything else, needs to be practiced if it's going to stick.

So what does that look like in practice? In my experience, the people who changed my trajectory the most didn't sugarcoat things or offer empty compliments. What they gave me was grounded belief. They saw potential, and they backed it up with real opportunity. That combination is what builds confidence.

To leave the right kind of mark, you also need to be willing to invest. Influence is not just about saying the right thing; it's about consistently doing the right thing. That means offering your time, creating space for someone to try, allowing room for failure, and staying close enough to help when things go sideways.

People don't grow just because you say you believe in them. They grow when you walk with them through the process.

I've often found that it helps to think about how someone once did that for me. I remember the people who trusted me with real responsibility before I had the experience to back it up. I remember what it felt like to be given a chance and what it meant to rise to the occasion. That kind of trust can transform a person. It doesn't guarantee success, but it does invite growth.

We need more of that kind of trust and belief, especially now.

We live in a world that loves fast feedback, quick wins, and instant validation. However, most people don't need more applause. They need real development. They need someone who is willing to tell them the truth and help them step up to the plate. That is where influence becomes lasting.

Leaving your mark begins with how you carry yourself. If you are still listening to the voices that tell you what you cannot do, you will inevitably end up projecting that fear onto the people you are trying to lead. The most effective mentors I have known have been those who dealt with their own doubts first. They didn't pretend to have it all figured out, but they didn't let fear run the show.

That's what I want to model for others now. I don't want to offer speeches or shortcuts. I want to offer the same kind of steady belief that once moved the needle for me.

You don't need a title or a stage to lead this way. You simply need to care enough to act. Look around. Pay attention.

Someone in your life is waiting to be believed in. Someone is trying to decide whether they belong in the room, whether they can take the next step, or whether they are worth the effort. Your influence might be the reason they decide to try.

You already know what it looks like to lead with belief. You've seen it before, and you've felt it in your own life. Now it's your turn to pass it on.

WHAT YOU LEAVE BEHIND

Every leader leaves a mark. Whether it's intentional or not, the way you carry yourself—how you speak, how you respond to pressure, and the way you treat other people—shapes the environment around you. That influence either builds people up or wears them down. It's never neutral.

The people who leave the deepest impact rarely do it through charisma or inspiration. They do it through consistency. They tell the truth. They set expectations. They give real responsibility before someone feels ready. And they don't lower the standard just to make things easier.

What they offer isn't advice. Instead, like my dad, the lesson they offer is an example to follow. It's not flashy. It's not complicated. But it works.

There's always a new method, a faster strategy, and a louder way to get attention. But when it comes to building people— actually developing them—the flash doesn't hold. What holds are the old-school lessons for life.

Outwork everyone. Overcome setbacks. Never stop learning. Bet on yourself. Make business personal. Develop an abundance mindset. Share your time. Be present. Play the long game. And finally, leave a mark that helps someone else move forward.

The further you go, the easier it is to drift from those core lessons. You get busy. You start measuring what's urgent instead of what's lasting. You forget how much the early moments mattered—when someone gave you a chance, held you to a higher standard, or simply made the time.

So take a moment to take stock of where you are. Ask yourself, *Who around me is learning how to lead by watching me?* What are you reinforcing in your day-to-day choices? Is it belief, or is it self-doubt? Are you helping people see what's possible, or are you just preparing them to play it safe?

Whether you realize it or not, the people around you aren't just following your directions; they're watching your example.

So keep the standard high. Push when it would be easier to step back. Give others the tools to grow and the opportunities to take responsibility for themselves. Speak confidence into them when it's uncomfortable. And be consistent when it's inconvenient.

You won't always see the payoff right away, but that's okay. Real influence compounds over time. It shows up later— sometimes long after you're gone—through the fingerprints you leave behind.

Whether you realize it or not, your fingerprints are already there.

Now's the time to make sure they're worth leaving.

NOTE OF GRATITUDE

Throughout the pages of this book, many people have had a profound impact on me, but one epitomizes the qualities and old-school values that made a critical impact on my journey—Mark B. Murphy. Mark is one of the most impressive, successful entrepreneurs and quality human beings I have had the opportunity to meet or work with throughout my life. If not for my dear friend Mark I would likely have never become an author in the first place, this being my third book.

Mark not only encouraged me to write my first two books but more importantly opened my mind to bigger and better thinking. He introduced me to Dan Sullivan, the legendary executive coach to entrepreneurs—"the Strategic Coach" who has made a huge impact not only on growing my business organization as an entrepreneur but providing me with powerful tools to help countless clients change their lives. In essence, Mark helped me take my existing positive mindset and belief in a bigger and brighter future in both life and business and put it on steroids.

Over the years, I shared many of the stories in this book with Mark, and when we were out socially, he always asked me to share the many stories about my dad with others. When I reflect, the truth is that I could have written every chapter in this book *and* included a story about Mark in each chapter. I thought I was the hardest-working person I knew (other than my father, of course) until I met Mark. He outworks everyone, turns setbacks into opportunities, is constantly learning new approaches and reinventing himself, and always invests in himself, his business, and his people. Mark makes all business intensely personal because he cares deeply about others, comes from abundance—never scarcity—and gives so freely of his time that he often leaves no time for himself. He makes you feel like you are the only person in the room, creating long-term success in favor of instant gratification, and most importantly, spending every day being a hero to others.

Today, Mark and I share many common clients as collaboration partners trying to be heroes to others, accomplishing much more together than we could separately. Most people know Mark as one of the nation's leading *Forbes*-rated financial advisors and wealth managers who helps many people build multigenerational wealth and a life by design. But I know him as the ultimate collaboration hero who spends his days helping as many people as he can achieve their dreams. I have been blessed to call him my friend, and I thank him for encouraging me to bring my dad's stories to life on the pages of this book and discuss what it means to be "Authentic."

Mark Murphy and me, December 2025

ABOUT THE AUTHOR

Bill Barrett has built a career defined by authenticity, trusted relationships, and strategic vision. An accomplished entrepreneur, corporate attorney, and CEO of Mandelbaum Barrett PC, he has guided hundreds of business owners through some of their most pivotal decisions—helping them navigate growth, transition, and legacy with confidence and clarity.

As the author of two previous books and host of the Fingerprints on Success podcast, Bill continues to explore what it means to lead with purpose, build with integrity, and create meaningful impact in business and life. In Authentic, he reflects on lessons learned through his own entrepreneurial journey, honoring timeless principles of leadership, trust, and living with intention.

To connect with Bill Barrett for speaking engagements, professional opportunities, or inquiries, contact WBarrett@ mblawfirm.com or (973) 243-7952.